Ivy League Programs at State School Prices

JOHN TOLLAN.

Ivy League Programs at State School Prices

Robert R. Sullivan
Professor, City University of New York
and
Karin R. Randolph

Prentice Hall
New York • London • Toronto • Sydney • Tokyo • Singapore

This book is dedicated to Luap and Nitsuj.

First Edition

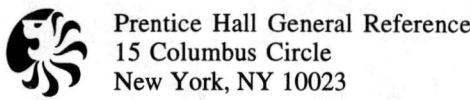

Prentice Hall General Reference
15 Columbus Circle
New York, NY 10023

Copyright © 1994 by Robert B. Sullivan and Karin R. Sullivan
All rights reserved
including the right of reproduction
in whole or in part in any form

An Arco Book

ARCO and PRENTICE HALL are registered trademarks
of Prentice-Hall, Inc.
Colophon is a trademark of Prentice-Hall, Inc.

Library of Congress Cataloging-in-Publication Data

Sullivan, Robert R.
    Ivy League programs at state school prices / Robert R. Sullivan.—
— 1st ed.
    p. cm.
    ISBN 0-671-87426-8
    1. Universities and colleges—United States—Honors courses—
Directories. I. Title. II. Title: Arco Ivy League programs at
state school prices.
LB2364.S85 1994
378.1'7942—dc20   93-49448
                            CIP

Manufactured in the United States of America

1 2 3 4 5 6 7 8 9 10

Contents

Colleges and Universities by State ix

How and Why to Read This Book xiii

Honors Programs *1*
    University of Alabama, Tuscaloosa 3
    University of Arizona 6
    University of Arkansas 9
    University of California, Irvine 12
    University of California, Los Angeles 15
    University of California, Riverside 18
    University of California, San Diego 22
    University of California, Santa Barbara 24
    University of Connecticut 27
    University of Delaware 29
    University of Florida 32
    University of Georgia 35
    University of Hawaii, Manoa 39

CONTENTS

    University of Idaho   42
    University of Illinois, Urbana–Champaign   44
    Indiana University   47
    University of Iowa   50
    University of Kansas   53
    University of Kentucky   56
    Louisiana State University   59
    University of Maryland   62
    University of Massachusetts at Amherst   65
    Miami University   69
    University of Michigan, Ann Arbor   71
    Michigan State University   74
    University of Minnesota   77
    University of Mississippi   81
    University of Missouri   84
    University of Montana   87
    University of Nevada–Reno   90
    University of New Hampshire   92
    University of New Mexico   95
    City University of New York   98
    State University of New York at Albany   102
    State University of New York at Buffalo   104
    State University of New York at Stony Brook   107
    University of North Carolina at Chapel Hill   110
    Ohio State University   113
    University of Oklahoma   116
    University of Oregon   119
    Pennsylvania State University   121
    Rutgers University   124
    University of Rhode Island   127
    University of South Carolina   130
    New College of the University of South Florida   134

CONTENTS

University of Tennessee *136*
University of Texas at Austin *140*
Texas A&M University *143*
University of Utah *146*
University of Virginia *149*
University of Washington *152*
West Virginia University *155*
College of William & Mary *158*
University of Wisconsin–Madison *161*
University of Wyoming *164*

COLLEGES AND UNIVERSITIES BY STATE

Alabama	University of Alabama, Tuscaloosa
Arizona	University of Arizona
Arkansas	University of Arkansas
California	University of California, Irvine
	University of California, Los Angeles
	University of California, Riverside
	University of California, San Diego
	University of California, Santa Barbara
Connecticut	University of Connecticut
Delaware	University of Delaware
Florida	University of Florida
	New College of the University of South Florida
Georgia	University of Georgia
Hawaii	University of Hawaii, Manoa
Idaho	University of Idaho

COLLEGES AND UNIVERSITIES BY STATE

Illinois	University of Illinois, Urbana–Champaign
Indiana	Indiana University
Iowa	University of Iowa
Kansas	University of Kansas
Kentucky	University of Kentucky
Louisiana	Louisiana State University
Maryland	University of Maryland
Massachusetts	University of Massachusetts at Amherst
Michigan	University of Michigan, Ann Arbor
	Michigan State University
Minnesota	University of Minnesota
Mississippi	University of Mississippi
Missouri	University of Missouri
Montana	University of Montana
Nevada	University of Nevada–Reno
New Hampshire	University of New Hampshire
New Jersey	Rutgers University
New Mexico	University of New Mexico
New York	City University of New York
	State University of New York at Albany
	State University of New York at Buffalo
	State University of New York at Stony Brook
North Carolina	University of North Carolina at Chapel Hill
Ohio	Miami University
	Ohio State University
Oklahoma	University of Oklahoma
Oregon	University of Oregon
Pennsylvania	Pennsylvania State University
Rhode Island	University of Rhode Island
South Carolina	University of South Carolina
Tennessee	University of Tennessee

COLLEGES AND UNIVERSITIES BY STATE

Texas	University of Texas at Austin
	Texas A&M University
Utah	University of Utah
Virginia	University of Virginia
	College of William & Mary
Washington	University of Washington
West Virginia	West Virginia University
Wisconsin	University of Wisconsin–Madison
Wyoming	University of Wyoming

HOW AND WHY
TO READ THIS BOOK

▶ This book is for academically talented high school juniors and seniors from families with moderate incomes. If you and your parents match this profile, you may be qualified for one or more honors programs at major state universities in the United States, and the meaning of this can be summed up in one phrase: quality education at low prices.

By academically talented we mean that you must have at least a straight B average in high school and at least an 1100 on the SAT or 26 on the ACT. If you meet these standards, you will qualify for a few of the honors programs described in this book. You will get small classes taught by full-time professors, something you do not often get at Ivy League universities. You may be able to afford these programs as well, for the total cost of attending a state university is usually less than half the total cost at an Ivy League university.

However, suppose you have compiled a better record than a straight B but still come from a family of moderate means. Let's say you have compiled an A− average or higher and have scored 1200 or above on the SAT, or 28 or above on the ACT. You will then qualify for several programs that are *better* than the regular programs at Ivy League institutions. You'll be surrounded by equally qualified students, something that does not always happen at the Ivies. You'll have full-time professors instead of teaching assistants (TAs), and you'll be in seminars of 12 to 20 students.

If, for example, you have an A− high school average and scored 1350 on the SAT, you may qualify for admission to the University of Texas honors program. It is one of the best in the nation, and the total (room, board, and tuition) cost for out-of-state residents is still under $9,000 annually. You'll get a better education than at Harvard and for one-third the price. If you have some doubts about Austin, Texas, and think that Ann Arbor, Michigan, is a better town, you may be right, but attending school there will cost you more. The University of Michigan also has one of the best honors programs in the United States, but for a total cost of about $16,000 annually, about two-thirds the cost of an Ivy. If you think that Ann Arbor is worth $9,000 annually (the difference between Texas and Michigan), then enroll in the University of Michigan's honors program.

But let's go back to where we started and say you are the last one through the elite door. You just managed a straight B average and received 1150 on the SAT. This is not bad, but all other things being equal, you most certainly would not get into an Ivy League school. However, you just might be admitted to the honors program at the University of Arkansas, which happens to be a good program at an inexpensive university. Fayetteville, Arkansas, is a charming town, the campus is beautiful, and the best professors are hungry for good students. There are another half-dozen programs like Arkansas' described in this book.

* * *

Let's retreat a few steps and answer the question of just what honors programs are. Almost always, they are educational programs that adhere to college-wide requirements but do so with smaller classes of select students, taught by the best professors and administered by an honors program staff. Such programs cost money. Cutting class size in half and bringing in full-time professors instead of teaching assistants (TAs) is *very* costly, which raises the question of why public universities sponsor honors programs. The answer is that they want to compete with the Ivies and bring in students who will enrich the entire campus, and there is no other way to do it than by providing an education equal to or better than you can get in the Ivy League. State universities consider the money spent for honors programs a good investment.

At this point, let's make a distinction between an *honors program* and an *honors college*. An honors program is basically linked to the mainstream of the university where it is located, and it is headed by a director. An honors college is usually a separate entity from the mainstream educational process, and it is most often headed by a dean. In an honors program, you take some small honors sections (how many and when are key questions), but most of your courses are taken with other students in normal sections. In an ideal honors college, you take all of your courses separately. In reality, there are few if any pure honors colleges, despite the titles. Most of what you will find at state universities are honors programs, and the critical issues concern how they are organized.

What distinguishes a good honors program from a mediocre one is *money*, or how much the university budgets for the program. This is too brief an answer, however, for money can be poorly spent or well spent. Therefore, we need a firmer rule, and for us in this book it is this: A good honors program at a state university is one that is *front-loaded*, meaning a program that spends its money on small classes in the first two years. This criterion can be explained by the following illustration.

Indiana University requires all freshmen to take two western civilization courses. A section of one of these courses usually includes 150 students and is taught by a full-time professor. If this constitutes one-third of that professor's teaching load, then it accounts for one-sixth of his or her salary cost, plus the cost of a TA and overhead. Let's say that's a total cost of $30,000, or roughly $200 per student. In the Honors Division, Indiana University runs several small sections of these courses, each averaging about 15 students. To round things off, let's stop at 10 seminars of H101, as it's called, for at this point we are dealing with 150 honors freshmen. No TAs are involved, but the overhead costs are higher, for the Honors Division has five full-time administrators. Suppose the aggregate cost is for *10* full-time professors to give the sections, plus the usual overhead expenses. The cost of running 10 such sections may then be well over $300,000, or 10 times the money spent on regular students! This is a *major* financial difference.

A questionable honors program is one that is *back-loaded*, meaning that most of the honors sections are provided in the last two years. The reason such a program is questionable is that the last two years at state universities are already a type of honors program. Classes are small, the worst students have departed, the faculty is full-time, and the student with a chosen major is a player of sorts in the smaller administrative setup of a department. Therefore, there are only marginal benefits to students in honors courses given in these two years. There is nothing wrong with honors courses in the last two years, but

HOW AND WHY TO READ THIS BOOK

if a university offers them only during this time (which is rare), the honors program is really somewhat illusory, for you get most of these benefits just by reaching the point of being an upperclass student with a major.

Now that we have sharply distinguished good from merely fair honors programs, allow us to soften the difference. Some honors programs provide small sections in the first two years but make them optional. We are queasy about this, but we do recognize it as a partial solution. Some honors programs back-load their requirements but then do well by their students by providing real seminars with 12 students instead of small lecture sections with 35. We do not think this is the best way to spend money, but if the budget is tight, it may be the only way. There are certainly worse ways to run an honors program.

Finally, much more goes into honors programs than these paragraphs indicate, but space constraints prevent us from going into further detail. This is a book about specific honors programs and not about honors programs in general, but we thought it would be a good idea to let you know that our approach toward these programs is as analytical as possible. With that much said, let us move on to the specifics of this book.

* * *

This book provides profiles of entry-level honors programs in flagship state universities in the United States. Our ground rule is to look at the liberal arts honors program in the major state university in most of the states. Most states have one flagship state university and a number of secondary state universities or state colleges. We have limited our search to the flagship state universities. That's the rule; now let us note the many exceptions.

The two largest states, California and New York, are exceptions to the rule of having one flagship campus in that each has several. In California, we look at UC Irvine, UC Los Angeles, UC Riverside, UC San Diego, and UC Santa Barbara. In New York, where the state university (SUNY) system is based on the California model, we look at SUNY Albany, SUNY Buffalo, and SUNY Stony Brook. We also look at the CUNY BA Program at the City University of New York. We make further exceptions for Florida, Ohio, Michigan, Texas, and Virginia, for these states' systems are characterized not only by quality flagship

HOW AND WHY TO READ THIS BOOK

universities but also by secondary universities that are either of exceptionally high quality or have exceptional honors programs. The programs in point are at the New College of the University of South Florida, Miami University in Ohio, the Honors College at Michigan State University, Texas A&M University, and William & Mary College in Virginia.

Other than these exceptions, we are consistent with our rule and look only at the flagship state university. For example, in Iowa we look at the honors program at the University of Iowa but not at Iowa State or the regional campuses of the state system. In Illinois we look at the University of Illinois in Urbana but not at Chicago Circle or at the regional campuses. In some states, we analyze no honors program either because there is none or because we felt that the program was too tenuous or of questionable quality. We are also incomplete in our coverage of flagship state universities because some did not respond or because we received their information too late.

There are two noteworthy omissions in this book, the University of California at Berkeley and the State University of New York at Binghamton. The reason for their omission is that they do not have honors programs. We were never able to find out precisely why this is the case at Berkeley, and at SUNY Binghamton, which is as high-quality a state university as one will find in the United States, an official told us that it is because the entire campus is considered to be a honors program.

* * *

Each honors program is looked at in terms of several categories that we think shed light on quality. The town and the campus are the social and physical settings of honors programs, and if these are not good, the program in question will be adversely affected. Such judgments are admittedly subjective. We acknowledge a fondness for Ann Arbor and the need to stifle a yawn when thinking of some other state university towns that will remain unnamed. Similarly with the campus: it may be pretty, but if it does not have a lively intellectual life, the honors program will be impoverished. We also think a lively campus is the result of real geographic, racial, and ethnic diversity in the student body, an issue we will say more about later.

Entrance requirements are, of course, of critical importance, but our effort has been to go beyond the numbers to try to find out what universities are really looking for. We also want to know whether entrance requirements are flexible. Many high school graduates do well on the SAT *or* in grades but not in both. A high SAT score and average high school grades are taken to be a sign of an underachiever, and a low SAT score coupled with high grades is a sign of an overachiever. We try to find out if weakness in one area can be compensated for in the other.

We also wanted to generate a statistical profile of the program being looked at. Most programs are gender-balanced, but we raise the issue anyway, and there are a few surprises. Many have affirmative action policies, but we try to look beyond policy statements to learn the actual breakdown among underrepresented minorities and to determine whether the demographics of the state university is ahead of or behind those of its own state. The State of Iowa, for example, is only 3 percent minority, but the University Honors program is 7 percent African-American, and we take this to be a sign, and not the only one, of a strongly liberal atmosphere in the program. This does not necessarily mean that African-Americans will feel comfortable in Iowa City, but they may be more comfortable there than in Oxford, Ohio, and we say so. If we are not specific on minority breakdowns, this is because we were not able to get specific information.

One statistic is particularly important: State universities can become inbred because of the predominance of in-state students, and this is especially the case in a small state. We therefore think it is important for an honors program to attract out-of-state and out-of-region students. The honors program at the University of Illinois is made up of 83 percent in-state students, and this does not compare well with the University of Michigan, which has long had a policy of attracting out-of-state students to add diversity to a student body that would otherwise be too homogeneous.

However, we try to be cautious in this matter: The University of Illinois is somewhat inbred but it has a high-quality student body because it draws heavily from the fine high schools of the Chicago suburbs. Neighboring Indiana University, by contrast, brings in more out-of-state students; but since it does not draw from a metropolis such as Chicago, its in-state students are more provincial and conservative. Yet Indiana compensates for this by having fewer engineering students than the University of Illinois. Indiana's engineers are at Purdue.

We are also concerned with a program's prestige on and off

HOW AND WHY TO READ THIS BOOK

campus, and we address this factor when we have sufficient information (which is hard to come by). Older honors programs have an advantage over newer ones in this respect, for their graduates are usually well placed in the state and its university system. In effect these programs have "Old Boy" and (more recently) "Old Girl" networks and they add to the overall quality of the program. One of the great advantages of private colleges and universities over their public counterparts lies in this networking. Prestige can also greatly affect admission to graduate schools.

Another important consideration about state university honors programs is housing and facilities. Some honors programs have their own buildings, which we feel is definitely a plus; some have honors dormitories; most have honors floors in regular dormitories, which can make a big difference in the quality of life for honors undergraduates. We include any information we could gather about these matters. We also want to note that we are sensitive to the democratic urge of state universities to spread the benefits of honors programs by voiding such exclusive entities as honors dormitories.

We are especially concerned with the cost, since it is the ratio of cost to quality that inspired this book. State universities almost always have different in-state and out-of-state tuition. But room and board is always the same for in-staters and out-of-staters, so we pay no attention to it. We also assume a uniform cost for books, room, and board throughout the United States. We concentrate on the tuition cost, for this is where the real difference lies. We offer the in- and out-of-state tuition rates in our information box for each university.

We have also included any information we could gather about *fees* at state universities, such as library fees, student activities fees, and laboratory fees. We assumed that these were insignificant or more or less uniform until we discovered that the University of Massachusetts has fees of over $3,000 annually. There are only a few other instances of such high fees, but we include this information anyway.

Despite the significance of cost, however, it does not enter into our overall evaluation of honors programs. We felt that our picture would be distorted if we gave the University of Michigan a lower evaluation because it is the most expensive state university in this book. We therefore decided to limit our evaluative criteria to educational factors.

As noted, we provide an information box at the beginning of every entry, the upper half of which contains vital statistics, while the

HOW AND WHY TO READ THIS BOOK

bottom half contains summary judgments. The statistical information speaks for itself, but the summary judgments require explanation, which can best be done using a spread sheet. The judgments range from excellent to fair, but it should be emphasized that there is no "poor." We are willing to say the programs are poor in quality where that is the case, but, much to our amazement, although some are better than others, we did not find a single poor-quality honors program in the United States. Our guess is that quality goes with the territory: honors programs are by definition superior educational programs.

Here are our categories with the range of possible judgments:

Town & Campus:	Excellent	Good	Fair
Intellectual Setting:	Excellent	Good	Fair
Entrance Requirements:	Very Competitive	Competitive	Easy
Program Quality:	Excellent	Good	Fair

By limiting ourselves to three judgmental categories, we are trying to avoid being too precise with programs that do not lend themselves to exact measurement. It should also be noted that the arrangement itself is keyed to these programs. For example, we think that there is no such thing as "open" admission to an honors program, but there are programs that are relatively easy, and this means that they accept an SAT score of 1100 to 1200. Rather than be overly specific, we just say "Easy."

A cautionary note is in order: We think that all the above categories are significant, and that *program quality* taken alone, is not determinative. A good program set on a nice campus in a town that is only *fair* may well end up providing a mediocre educational experience. A *good* program is well organized and carefully administered, with individualized opportunities, and much, much more. But if such a program is in only a *fair* intellectual setting, the participating student may end up feeling impoverished.

And finally we come to the most difficult category of all. This is the composite category that we have called *Overall Evaluation*. Here we have used a three-star system of our own devising. A few universities have superb programs in great towns on beautiful campuses alive with intellectual life and at a cost which is beyond belief. These programs receive three stars, and there are 13 of them. It should be

HOW AND WHY TO READ THIS BOOK

reiterated that *cost* is not a factor in this overall evaluation; it is rather the judgment of the program and its context.

We want to note that the majority of programs received two stars for reasons that might not seem relevant to the reader: On the anticipated bell-shaped curve, most universities ended up with two, fewer got three, and even fewer got one star. In defense of these few that got one star, we should emphasize that they are *good* programs, not bad; had they been bad, they would not have been included. We also want to add that those with one star may even be excellent for subjective reasons that matter only to the individual reader. For example, often a one-star program cannot attract superior students, but precisely this situation may provide opportunities for students with relatively low SAT scores who thought they could never get into an honors program.

* * *

We initially telephoned universities across the nation to solicit printed information about their honors programs, often having informative conversations, and we collected background data about state universities from various sources, including the student guides now on the market. To some hard-to-determine extent, our information is firsthand and has been gathered over the past 20 years from visits to various campuses.

We then telephoned honors programs and conducted lengthy interviews, usually from 45 to 60 minutes with their officers. We often followed up with additional calls to, for example, the university's institutional research office to get statistics. Separate calls were made to bursars' offices for financial information. Where possible, we crosschecked our impressions with faculty (and occasionally students) at the universities in question. Finally, we sent out drafts (without the first and last paragraphs or the information box) to program directors and asked them to proof them for errors and omissions and return them by a specified date. Nevertheless, we cannot guarantee that there will not be errors.

We are also well aware that some program directors will disagree with our evaluations. The hardest part of this project has been making judgments, but we felt that this was also the most valuable part. Where directors can make reasoned and unbiased cases against our judgments, we invite them to do so.

Most important, in deference to Aristotle, we have tried to

HOW AND WHY TO READ THIS BOOK

analyze honors programs in terms appropriate to them, and these terms, or categories, are by no means the rigorous terms of mathematics. In other words, we think we have attained a level of objectivity appropriate to our materials. But having done this, we must point out that the high school seniors and parents reading this book are trying to make customized decisions for real individuals. This is the one thing we cannot do in this book.

Hence, even though a program like that at the University of Texas at Austin may well rate three stars by our standards, this does not mean that it is the best program for you. If you have the money, Michigan might be better, or if you are strongly inclined to research, Penn State might be better than both Texas or Michigan. But then again you might want to stay close to home, and so you might prefer the University of Georgia or Arkansas, both good programs according to our categories. You know your reasons and we do not, and your needs should be given their due weight when everything is thrown onto the scale.

Finally, a word or two about the author of this book and his credentials. I am a tenured full professor teaching political science at the City University of New York. I am a member of two doctoral faculties and have published about 25 articles and review articles in refereed journals, written one book published by a university press, and translated a book published by a second university press. I have taught in my home college's honors program, but more significantly, I spent a good deal of my three-year term as department chair thinking and arguing about undergraduate education. Perhaps most significant of all, I began writing this book at the time my second son was a senior in high school, and I am pleased to say that he is presently happily esconced in one of the honors programs described in this book. So I think it might reasonably be said that I am one of the parents for whom this book was written.

Robert R. Sullivan
New York City

HONORS PROGRAMS

UNIVERSITY OF ALABAMA, TUSCALOOSA	
PROGRAM:	University Honors Program
DIRECTOR:	Dr. Ralph Bogardus
SECRETARY:	Ms. Shirley Culp
ADDRESS:	University Honors Program Box 870169 Tuscaloosa, AL 35487-0169
TELEPHONE:	(205) 348-5500
TUITION (FEES):	**IN-STATE** $1,508 ($500) **OUT-OF-STATE** $4,516 ($500)
TOWN & CAMPUS:	Fair
INTELLECTUAL SETTING:	Fair
ENTRANCE REQUIREMENTS:	Competitive
PROGRAM QUALITY:	Good
OVERALL EVALUATION:	★★

▶ The University of Alabama at Tuscaloosa is best known for its football team, the Crimson Tide. Until 10 years ago there was nothing much else to say about Bama, but in recent years the university has become much better academically. Still, it is not the intellectual center of the new South. It is strongest in business and engineering, and lags somewhat in the humanities and the natural sciences. Extracurricular intellectual life is also not Alabama's strong suit. Socializing and partying is, and such extracurricular activities take place both on campus and on the Strip in downtown Tuscaloosa.

Admission to the University Honors Program is fairly selective. Applicants should have an ACT score of 28 or better, or at least 1220 on the SAT. Applicants are also expected to have a good high school GPA.

A brief essay is also required. National Merit Finalists, National Achievement Finalists, University of Alabama Presidential Scholars, and Alumni Honors Scholars are automatically admitted to the Honors Program. For this year's entering freshman class, the average ACT score was 30 and the average SAT score was 1250.

IVY LEAGUE PROGRAMS AT STATE SCHOOL PRICES

The basic structure of the Honors Program is called the *Honors Division*. Here students take a three-hour General Honors Survey and 15 additional hours of honors courses, one of which may be honors thesis work. A variation on this theme is the *Special Honors Division*, in which students take *two* three-hour General Honors Survey courses, 15 additional hours of honors courses, *and* an additional course of honors thesis work. In effect, the Honors Division requires 18 hours of honors course work and the Special Honors Division 24 hours.

Honors students take one or two honors courses every semester in small sections taught by full-time faculty. Students may apply up to six credits of departmental honors courses plus three credits for the departmental honors thesis toward the honors program. Those doing Special Honors may apply up to nine departmental honors credits as well as three credits for the departmental honors thesis. These so-called departmental honors courses originate in only three departments, so they are not a significant factor in the Honors Program.

One positive feature of the University Honors Program is its location in Temple Tutwiler Hall, which could not be closer to the center of the campus. Administrative offices are located here, as is a small library, three conference rooms, and a lounge with national newspapers and magazines.

There are a total of 550 students in the University Honors Program, and approximately 115 new freshmen are admitted each year. Women make up 46 percent of the total number of students, and minorities make up about 8 percent. African-Americans are less than 5 percent of the program's participants. There are roughly 125 out-of-state students in the program, most of whom come from neighboring states.

Some scholarship aid is available for honors students at the University of Alabama, mainly from sources such as the Alabama Presidential Scholars and the Alumni Honors Scholars programs. About 60 percent of Alabama honors students are on scholarships that provide at least tuition money. The good news from Alabama is that the Honors Program is participating in a five-year capital fund-raising campaign and the first year has been very successful. Hence, more scholarship money will be available in the future.

Special housing for honors students is available. There is an honors dormitory for men, Byrd Hall, and another, Fitts Hall, for women. Housing at the University of Alabama is said to be good.

Alongside the regular Honors Program is a smaller program called the Computer-Based Honors Program (CBHP). The director is Dr. Kathy Randall, and her telephone number is (205) 348-5029. This program is designed for students who want to incorporate computer work into their majors, which may be anything but computer science. Freshmen begin with an intensive course in computer basics, where they are introduced to at least two computer languages and to practical problem-solving. Once they have gained facility, they normally go on to work with a faculty member whose interests coincide with theirs. Each week in the sophomore through senior years, CBHP students meet with each other in a seminar to exchange ideas and compare experiences.

The CBHP was cited as one of the most innovative honors programs in the United States by the National Council of Honors Programs. The National Institute of Education said of the program that it represents a classic case of institutional change driven by student achievement, referring to the accomplishments of a few students in the 1960s that forced the institution to recognize that it had to build a program to continue what had been begun. Only 20 students are accepted yearly, and their average ACT score is 32, which translates to about 1350 on the SAT.

On balance, the Honors Program at the University of Alabama is good and in many respects outstanding. The problem is its context. Alabama is a poor state, and students at the University tend to be something less than the best. But if one has the specific goal of entering the Computer-Based Honors Program or the regular Honors Program because it is expanding, then Alabama might be a good place to go. ■

UNIVERSITY OF ARIZONA

PROGRAM:	The Honors Center
DIRECTOR:	Dr. Clifford M. Lytle
ASSOCIATE DIRECTOR:	Dr. Richard Kissling
ADDRESS:	The Honors Center Slonaker House (Rm. 107) The University of Arizona Tucson, AZ 85721
TELEPHONE:	(602) 621-6901
TUITION (FEES):	**IN-STATE** $1,844 (incl.) **OUT-OF-STATE** $7,350 (incl.)
TOWN & CAMPUS:	Good
INTELLECTUAL SETTING:	Fair
ENTRANCE REQUIREMENTS:	Competitive
PROGRAM QUALITY:	Good
OVERALL EVALUATION:	★★

▶ The University of Arizona is the quintessential Sunbelt campus: southwestern architecture, all of 37,000 students, palm trees, rolling lawns, endless cars, distant mountains, and of course a sun that always cooperates. It makes for an atmosphere more conducive to play than serious study, and to some extent this is the case. There are nonetheless good departments, and, as might be expected, the astronomy department is one of the best in the nation. Optical Sciences is also good, as are Anthropology and Creative Writing. Yet despite growth and excellent prospects, this is not the intellectual center that UCLA or UC Berkeley are in the PAC 10.

Entrance requirements to the Honors Center are competitive, but, fortunately, are simple and clear. Applicants must be in the top 5 percent of their high school graduating classes *or* have SAT scores of at least 1300 (30 on the ACT). These standards are minimum and few exceptions are made.

The Arizona program tends to be back-loaded, by which we mean that there are no express underclass requirements, even though there is encouragement by advisors to take honors courses in the first two years. What requirements there are will be found concentrated in the upperclass years. Normally, back-loading is an indicator that the program is underfunded or that the university is downsizing or cost-cutting, but this may not be the case at Arizona. Placement tests are given to incoming freshmen, and through these, many are routed into honors sections of English composition, math, and foreign language courses.

In order to graduate with honors, students are required to take 30 credits of honors courses, six of which must be in the Honors Thesis sequence in the senior year. Students are also required to maintain a 3.5 GPA while in the program. But only about one-third of honors students pursue this option. The remainder simply take any honors courses they want and benefit from the environment the program provides.

Thus there is strong incentive to take some honors courses in the underclass years, and program advisors encourage students to take one or two courses a semester during this time. Roughly 75 percent of freshman honors students do in fact take at least one honors course per term. This is facilitated by the large number of honors sections that are offered each year. The Arizona brochure says that more than 200 honors courses are offered yearly, including 38 separate sections of honors freshman composition.

Honors courses are kept small, with an average class size of 15 students. They are mainly (but not completely) limited to honors students and are taught by full-time faculty, but these teachers are chosen by department chairs rather than by the Honors Center. The Honors Center does, however, try to cultivate professors with good reputations.

There are 2,000 students enrolled in the Honors Center program, making it one of the largest in the United States. Of this total, 51 percent are women, 20 percent are minorities, and 12 percent are from out of state. Honors students are encouraged to live in one of two recently renovated dormitories near the center of campus, and they are granted graduate student status at the university library. There is a strong honors advisement system in place, and students are organized in an Honors Student Association. The program encourages students to compete for prestigious national scholarships and has had impressive results in the past few years.

IVY LEAGUE PROGRAMS AT STATE SCHOOL PRICES

The University of Arizona is not expensive. In-state students pay $1,844 a year, a remarkably low figure. Out-of-state students pay $7,350 annually, also not expensive.

On balance, the Honors Center program at the University of Arizona is good, maybe even very good. Tucson is not Madison, Ann Arbor, or Berkeley in terms of the intellectual life on and around campus, however, and this is the main overall weakness of the program. ■

UNIVERSITY OF ARKANSAS

PROGRAM:	Honors Studies
DIRECTOR:	Prof. Elizabeth Payne
PROGRAM COORDINATOR:	Dr. Suzanne McCray
ADDRESS:	Honors Studies J. William Fulbright College of Arts & Sciences Old Main 517 University of Arkansas Fayetteville, AR 72701
TELEPHONE:	(501) 575-2509
TUITION (FEES):	**IN-STATE** $919 (incl.) **OUT-OF-STATE** $2,359 (incl.)
TOWN & CAMPUS:	Good
INTELLECTUAL SETTING:	Fair
ENTRANCE REQUIREMENTS:	Easy
PROGRAM QUALITY:	Good
OVERALL EVALUATION:	★★

▶ Fayetteville is a pretty town, and the campus is charming. But Arkansas is a poor state, and this is reflected in the middling quality of the student body of about 14,000, who are wild about football, keen on partying, and oriented toward business after graduation. There is nothing outstanding about intellectual life on campus. English is nonetheless a strong major at Arkansas, as is architecture.

Entrance requirements for Honors Studies at the J. William Fulbright College of Arts and Sciences are flexible. Desired is a high school GPA of 3.5 or better, an SAT score of at least 1100 (28 on the ACT), and a standing in the top 10 percent of one's high school graduating class. Students who are minimally qualified or fall slightly short are conditionally accepted for departmental honors rather than for the four-year honors program, but in practice they are part of the honors program and with motivation may share in its benefits.

There are 425 students in the Honors Studies program. Of these, about 60 graduate per year, and 15 of these graduates are four-year fellows. Last year, 102 freshmen were admitted, but only five of these students had ACT scores under 28 (SAT scores under 1150). The average ACT score for all students in the program was 31 (about 1290 on the SAT).

The program itself is unusual. One must complete the university requirements for graduation, but the courses taken need not be in honors. For example, six credits of freshman composition are required, but not necessarily in honors composition courses. Instead, honors students must take a special honors core curriculum, adding up to 51 credits of course work in arts and humanities, social sciences, natural sciences and mathematics, and foreign languages. The program is loosely structured, but the credit requirement is so high that it effectively makes the program front-loaded.

Freshmen are encouraged to take three honors courses per term, as are sophomores, for a total of 36 honors credits by the junior year. Juniors continue by taking honors colloquia, which are smaller sections of from 10 to 15 students. Roughly 15 hours of colloquia are required, and these apply toward the overall 51-credit minimum. Finally, upper juniors must begin a thesis, which is a written work of 40 to 50 pages that is defended orally before a committee.

Women make up 55 percent of the honors student body at the University of Arkansas. The number of minorities, specifically African-Americans, is said to be low, roughly around 2 percent, and 22 percent of students are from out of state. Honors housing is provided but not required. The Honors Center on the fifth floor of Old Main provides a lounge, kitchen, and computer room where students may meet.

The University of Arkansas is very inexpensive. Tuition for in-state students is $919 annually, and for out-of-state students it is $2,359. This is good news, but the really great news is that almost all honors students are on scholarship. In-state students receive tuition waivers and if they maintain a GPA of 3.25 or above, scholarships are automatically renewed. Out-of-state students are also predominantly on scholarship, and 10 of 20 Sturgis fellowships, each worth $10,000 annually, are given to out-of-state honors students, and are renewable for four years.

The University of Arkansas is dedicated to establishing the prestige of its program. Upon graduation, the completion of the honors program is noted on the student's transcript, all subsequent correspondence from the university concerning the graduate mentions this achievement, and at graduation the student is individually honored.

Honors Studies at the University of Arkansas presents an unusual opportunity. The university seems to provide the best program it can, but for reasons beyond its control, it is limited in the quality of students it can attract. It therefore offers a superb opportunity for the out-of-state student who would not make it into the honors programs at Penn State or Michigan or even Indiana or Rutgers but wants the advantages of an honors program. If you have a cumulative B+ GPA from high school, at least an 1150 on the SAT, and are from one of the northeastern or midwestern states, this is a good opportunity to get a fine education. ■

UNIVERSITY OF CALIFORNIA, IRVINE

PROGRAM:	Campuswide Honors Program
DIRECTOR:	Dr. Roger McWilliams
ASSOCIATE DIRECTOR:	Dr. Audrey DeVore
HONORS ADVISOR:	Ms. Susan Csikesz
ADDRESS:	Campuswide Honors Program Dean of Undergraduate Studies 256 Administration Building University of California Irvine, CA 92715-9788
TELEPHONE:	(714) 856-5461
TUITION (FEES):	IN-STATE: $3,074 (incl.) OUT-OF-STATE: $10,773 (incl.)
TOWN & CAMPUS:	Fair
INTELLECTUAL SETTING:	Fair
ENTRANCE REQUIREMENTS:	Competitive
PROGRAM QUALITY:	Fair
OVERALL EVALUATION:	★

▶ The University of California, Irvine (UCI), is located along the California coastline in Orange County, 40 miles south of Los Angeles. It is a new campus of low-rise buildings, with a total enrollment of 35,000 students. Intellectual and social life are said to be dull, and there are reasons for this. The atmosphere of the campus is preprofessional, with an unusually large number of premed students and others majoring in the sciences, especially biology, who intend to earn PhDs in their fields. Most come from southern California, and many commute from nearby LA and the LA suburbs.

Entrance requirements are competitive. The UCI Campuswide Honors Program (CHP) admits high school seniors who have attained at least a 3.5 cumulative high school GPA (on a 4.0 scale). The average GPA in recent freshmen classes was 4.1 (weighted to take account of Advanced Placement courses), and the average SAT score was 1300.

In addition, UCI requires all applicants to have taken three College Board Achievement Exams: English, Mathematics, and a third field of the student's choosing.

Application should be made to the University, and the deadline is in November. From the general pool of successful applicants, the CHP draws a specific pool of qualified honors candidates, who then go through a second filter of admissions committees representing each of the eight schools that make up UCI. The CHP then tries to choose numbers of students that reflect the enrollment distribution in the eight schools. About 20 percent of honors students study biological sciences in one of UCI's best schools. About 12 percent are in humanities, and another 20 percent are in the social sciences.

All first-year honors students take the yearlong Humanities Core Course in civilization. This is basically western civilization, but increasingly the course is being restructured to reflect contemporary concerns. The course focuses on history, literature, and philosophy, and emphasizes critical and creative thinking and writing. All second- and third-year honors students also take yearlong honors courses in the social sciences and the natural sciences. Finally, every fourth-year student takes a yearlong research course that involves doing a senior thesis or creative project within his or her major field of study.

The first three of the above core honors courses satisfy UCI breadth, or general education, requirements. They are given in small sections and taught by full-time faculty, and together they constitute the minimum number of courses one must take to graduate with the honors designation.

Like many modern universities, UCI is more a multiversity than a university, a phenomenon that is reflected in the proliferation of discipline-specific honors programs piggybacked to the core honors curriculum sketched above. In effect, this amounts to taking an honors program within one's major, and if these departmental honors programs differ at UCI, it is because they are more precisely described and coordinated by the honors administration.

Out-of-state tuition at UCI is relatively high, and in-state tuition is not low. There are a large number of scholarships available, and honors students are in a good position to win many of them. Out-of-state students should contact the UCI Office of Financial Aid regarding scholarships and be aware that the deadline for most applications is November 30. About 50 percent of honors students receive Regents scholarships, but unfortunately these have remained fixed at $500 while tuition and fees have steadily climbed.

There are 350 students in the UCI Campuswide Honors Program, and each year's incoming freshman class totals about 100. Of these, 50 percent are women and 20 percent are underrepresented minorities (not including Asian-Americans). This year's freshman class includes four African-Americans and 10 Hispanics. Out-of-state students make up only a small percentage of the total, and they are mainly from inland western states, such as Utah.

Many UCI students commute, but campus housing is plentiful. It should be emphasized that because of the strong commuting student contingent and the strong preprofessional atmosphere, living in the UCI dormitories is not one of life's great pleasures. This situation may change, however, as UCI is now building small-scale campus housing that may be quite attractive. In the fall of 1993, three 12-person houses for honors students were opened, and if they prove successful, UCI may well build more.

The Campuswide Honors Program at UCI presents a mixed picture. On the positive side, the honors program itself is well structured and administered and, although minimal, offers a good alternative to the large lecture sections characteristic of state universities. If one is interested in premed studies or in the biological sciences leading to a PhD, then UCI is a place worth looking into. The downside is that UCI is not at all an exciting place, either socially or intellectually, nor, if one is not majoring in the hard sciences, is it an especially strong institution. ■

PROGRAM:	Honors Programs
DIRECTOR:	Asst. Dean G. Jennifer Wilson
DIRECTOR OF COUNSELING:	Ms. Alison Nickerson
ADDRESS:	UCLA Honors Programs LS-10 College of Letters & Science 405 Hilgard Avenue Los Angeles, CA 90024-1414
TELEPHONE:	(310) 825-1553
TUITION (FEES):	**IN-STATE** $3,913 (incl.) **OUT-OF-STATE** $11,612 (incl.)
TOWN & CAMPUS:	Good
INTELLECTUAL SETTING:	Excellent
ENTRANCE REQUIREMENTS:	Very Competitive
PROGRAM QUALITY:	Excellent
OVERALL EVALUATION:	★ ★ ★

▶ The University of California, Los Angeles, or UCLA, is certainly a mixed package. Mainly a commuter college, it is clearly better in the sciences than in the liberal arts, and the students at UCLA are not as good as those at UC Berkeley. The campus and location demand that one have a car. The financial outlook is not good, for the State of California is suffering more than any other state from the current recession, and the entire university system is being hit hard. The cost of living around the UCLA campus is also very high. Yet for all that, UCLA is an exciting place to be. The cultural life on campus is excellent, and the city is very dynamic.

There are several honors programs managed by the Honors Programs office at UCLA. We are only interested in the largest one, called *College Honors*. Everything we say hereinafter is about this program.

Entrance requirements for incoming freshmen are very competitive. UCLA is looking for a high school GPA of at least 3.85 and an SAT score of 1300 or higher (or an ACT score of 31 or higher). Alternatively, one may gain entrance to the program by being in the top 3 percent of one's high school graduating class, and minorities may gain entrance through the affirmative action program. The average high school GPA of students in the program is about 4.0, which is a weighted average reflecting Advanced Placement courses taken. The average SAT score is said to be around 1300.

We asked UCLA officials whether they are flexible on these requirements, and they indicated that they are. Students not qualifying in one of the two areas stated above may appeal, and within reason there is a good chance of success.

The Honors Collegium is a collection of courses (about 12 new thematic offerings each quarter) that is taught by a small team of faculty in an interdisciplinary manner to small groups of students. Most Honors Collegium courses will satisfy general education, or core, requirements.

Accompanying specified Honors Collegium courses is a parallel set of skills courses that emphasize writing. Students must learn clear and graceful expression that meets the demands of the corresponding Honors Collegium courses. Only one or two of these courses are offered each quarter. The writing supplement will satisfy the core requirement for English composition.

Students are also free to choose from a long list of honors courses covering a wide range disciplines. For example, 17 anthropology courses were offered in academic year 1992–93. In addition to the Honors Collegium, the Honors Program oversees a series of honors discussion sections open only to honors students.

The requirements for College Honors are flexible and are worked out with a counselor, but in general the following may be said: students admitted to the program are automatically accepted to Plan A, which emphasizes course work, or they may select Plan B, which is research-oriented and features less course work. Essentially, the difference between Plan A and Plan B is whether or not one does a senior thesis.

UCLA measures student progress in terms of units (credits), and it is expected that students who have made a certain amount of progress (e.g., 72–107 units) will have included a certain number of honors units (e.g., 16) corresponding to that level of progress. Student progress is reviewed periodically. To complete the requirements of the College Honors Program, students must take 44 units of honors courses of the 180 units required to graduate from UCLA.

Students accepted into the Honors Program are put on a priority list that virtually guarantees a place in the dormitories, or residence halls, as they are called. In fact, all new students at UCLA are at the moment guaranteed housing, so there is no need to worry on this account. There is no honors-specific housing, however.

There are a number of scholarships available, including some university-wide scholarships, but we have no information about how many honors students receive them. There is also about $60,000 in honors-designated scholarship money, but it is awarded for achievement while at UCLA rather than in high school, which means that this money is available only after the freshman year.

Each year, about 750 new freshmen are brought into the College Honors Program, which includes roughly 2,000 students. Of these, 51 percent are women, and 47 percent are minorities. African-Americans make up 1 percent of the total, Hispanics are another 7 percent, and 35 percent are Asian-Americans. Out-of-state students comprise about 6 percent of the total number of honors students, and this is a declining figure, reflecting the fact that the state is tightening up its residency requirements. The days of claiming California resident status one year after entrance into the University of California are over.

The best aspects of the UCLA program are its students, who are of exceptional quality, the Honors Collegium, especially when it is reinforced by the writing seminars, and the fast-paced city of Los Angeles. For some, Los Angeles may be a drawback, as may the facts that UCLA is for the most part a commuter campus and the surrounding area is expensive. All of this taken together makes UCLA a mixed package, so good judgment is necessary. But it has an excellent honors program, make no mistake about that. ■

UNIVERSITY OF CALIFORNIA, RIVERSIDE

PROGRAM:	University Honors Program
DIRECTOR:	Prof. Alexander Rosenberg
ASSOCIATE DIRECTOR:	Dr. Kathleen Harris
ADDRESS:	University Honors Program 2672 Statistics-Computer University of California, Riverside Riverside, CA 92521-0108
TELEPHONE:	(909) 787-5323
TUITION (FEES):	IN-STATE $3,747 (incl.) OUT-OF-STATE $11,445 (incl.)
TOWN & CAMPUS:	Fair
INTELLECTUAL SETTING:	Fair
ENTRANCE REQUIREMENTS:	Competitive
PROGRAM QUALITY:	Good
OVERALL EVALUATION:	★★

▶ UC Riverside does not have a good reputation among California students, but its drawbacks are irrelevant to a good academic program, and academically, UC Riverside has a lot to offer. Unfortunately, the town of Riverside is dull, the campus architecture is uninteresting, there are no intercollegiate sports, and UC Riverside is said to be everyone's second choice in the California system. However, although all of this may be true, the faculty and curriculum (both general and honors) are excellent, the support services are superb, the intramural sports are great, and the student body is remarkably cohesive, with few people transferring out. UC Riverside could benefit from an aggressive public relations effort.

Entrance requirements to the University Honors Program (UHP) are competitive. Desired are a high school GPA of 3.7 or above, an SAT score of 1250 or above, and an essay that highlights the unique characteristics of the applicant. In fact, the average high school GPA is 4.11, an amazing number which is accounted for by factoring in Advanced Placement results. The average SAT score is 1231, but scores range from 1000 to 1470, indicating that UC Riverside is very flexible when evaluating an applicant's record.

The UHP is divided into two distinct parts, so mutually independent that qualified students may do the second (or upper division) half without having done the first (or lower division). We will take each in turn, but before moving on to the details, it should be pointed out that the UHP at Riverside is decidedly research-oriented and is designed to attract and cultivate students who will continue on to graduate school to earn PhDs. This orientation raises some interesting questions, but we will defer them until after having looked at the program.

Freshmen are first required to take Freshman Honors Research and Colloquium. This is a collective research experience in which groups of six freshmen are paired with a sophomore honors student and a faculty advisor. Students get organized and acquainted in the fall quarter and enroll in Honors 10-A in the winter quarter, when they divide work among themselves on a shared research topic. Each student writes a five-page background paper that serves as the foundation for the spring quarter, when students enroll in Honors 10-B and pool their individual work to produce a team product.

Freshmen are also required to take two additional honors courses, and the UHP administrators urge students to take two seminars/projects. These are small group meetings where faculty present their own projects, which are usually also research efforts. Very often these courses do double duty by satisfying core requirements, thereby allowing students to take more electives. Students may instead select courses from a list of honors sections, but the URP discourages this if it is done at the expense of the seminars/projects.

Sophomores are required to take two sophomore-level Honors Seminars that are distinguished from their freshman counterparts by greater emphasis on conceptualization.

This under-class experience is constructed as a supplement to the core, or general education, requirements. Core requirements are normally content-oriented rather than research-oriented, and it is difficult to mix the two. UC Riverside resolves the problem by not even attempting to do so. Needless to say, this means that the research experience is not in the least compromised.

The upper division of the UC Riverside program is also research-oriented. Students must apply for admission, but those who have completed lower-division honors have a good chance of being accepted. Not much is done in the junior year, as it is expected that students will concentrate on getting their majors on a solid footing. But juniors are also expected to be thinking about their senior thesis, for that is the heart and soul of the upper-division program.

The senior thesis is administered by a committee of faculty and is closely monitored by a faculty supervisor. The project itself is required to be substantive and independent. The former term indicates that the project should be demanding enough to warrant three or four credits for two or three quarters, or that it should equal the work done in two college courses. The requirement that the work be independent means that it must be both conceived and executed by the student. The student must neither be a mere research assistant on a preconceived project nor, having conceived a project, fail to follow through.

One of the most attractive features of the UC Riverside Honors Program is that it serves as a direct pipeline into the university's biomedical sciences program. This in turn provides direct access to the UCLA Medical School. Students are forewarned, however, that since UC Riverside does not want to abuse its privileged relationship with UCLA Medical School, its own biomedical sciences program is made especially difficult to get through. Hence, admission is no guarantee of success.

Each year 50 to 75 new freshmen are accepted into a program in which there are a total of 350 students, 130 in the lower division and 220 in the upper division. Of these, 47 percent are women, 22 percent are underrepresented minorities, namely, African-Americans (4 percent of the total) and Hispanics (18 percent of the total).

Only 5 percent of the students in the UC Honors Program are from out of state. This is to be expected because California is a large and populous state, and its surrounding states are relatively unpopulated. Because it is also a diverse state, the diversity brought by the out-of-state population to the UHP is less significant than it might be elsewhere.

Out-of-state tuition and fees at UC Riverside is $11,445, and in-state tuition is $3,747. What must be remembered about this as well as other California institutions is that the state is in a severe economic squeeze at the moment and colleges and universities are being asked to cut costs and downsize. Tuition may be going up while services are going down. Scholarship funds may be smaller now than they were in the golden 1980s.

There is no specific honors housing at UC Riverside, and there is a housing shortage on campus, but we were told that honors students are taken care of and should expect to have no problems finding housing.

On balance, the University Honors Program at UC Riverside is very well suited to the high school senior who thinks that he or she might like to become a researcher or go on to medical school. It is nicely front-loaded, emphasizing *methods* courses rather than *content* courses. Students are well prepared to do the senior thesis, and, when this is accomplished, well prepared for graduate school. Thus, this research-oriented program is particularly good despite the less-than-desirable reputation of UC Riverside. It is a good alternative to the Penn State program, and easier to get into as well. ■

UNIVERSITY OF CALIFORNIA, SAN DIEGO

PROGRAM:	Thurgood Marshall College Honors Program
DIRECTOR:	Ms. Mae Brown
ASSOCIATE DIRECTOR:	Ms. Ann Porter
ADDRESS:	Thurgood Marshall Honors Program University of California, San Diego 9500 Gilman Drive La Jolla, CA 92093-0509
TELEPHONE:	(619) 534-4110
TUITION (FEES):	**IN-STATE** $3,642 (incl.) **OUT-OF-STATE** $11,340 (incl.)
TOWN & CAMPUS:	Good
INTELLECTUAL SETTING:	Good
ENTRANCE REQUIREMENTS:	Very Competitive
PROGRAM QUALITY:	Fair
OVERALL EVALUATION:	★

▶ UC San Diego is a functional campus located practically on the beach and not very far from the Mexican border. It has long had a good reputation as a research university, and its undergraduates tend to continue their education, going on to medical school, law school, or graduate programs culminating in the PhD. Like all other units of the California system, UC San Diego has been hard hit by budget cuts but still provides a solid education.

Organized in terms of five colleges that provide separate housing and academic emphases, UC San Diego is known as an intellectually serious place. Thurgood Marshall College, formerly called Third College, is the unit most sharply focused on liberal arts.

Entrance requirements to the Thurgood Marshall College Honors Program (TMCHP) are very competitive. The admissions committee first looks for an evaluated high school GPA of 3.8 or higher, which means a solid A− average in a solid array of college preparatory courses. Secondly, TMCHP expects an SAT score of at least 1300, with no lower than a 650 in each component. The latter

UNIVERSITY OF CALIFORNIA, SAN DIEGO

requirement is a sure sign of an emphasis on liberal arts, for it indicates a desire on the part of TMCHP to ensure that students are verbally adept.

The TMCHP works along the following lines: At its center is an honors seminar on topical issues. It meets every Tuesday afternoon. Affiliated with the seminar is a program of outside speakers, such as Marian Wright Edelman, President of the Children's Defense Fund, and Dr. Sidney Wolfe, Director of Ralph Nader's Health Care Reform Team, who generally stay overnight on campus. The students usually read writings by these speakers and interact with them. Other than these seminars and the departmental honors courses, there are no formal honors courses, and the only honors requirement is that students maintain a 3.5 GPA over their undergraduate careers.

There are about 200 students in the TMCHP, and about 20 new freshmen are admitted each year. Minorities, including Asian-Americans, account for 37 percent of the students. Only a very small percentage of honors students are from out of state. In-state students tend to be from all over California. No statistics on women are available.

There are a number of university-wide scholarships, and students who qualify for admission to the TMCHP are in a very good position to get them. Regents Scholarships vary from $2,500 to $12,000. Alumni Scholarships provide room, board, and tuition and are renewable for four years. Applicants should be aware that the scholarship application is part of the application procedure. Make sure you are filing the correct forms, and if you are not certain, check with the UCSD Scholarship Office at (619) 534-3263.

There is no special honors housing at Thurgood Marshall College, but there are dormitories, and there is no problem in getting a place in one of them.

On balance, the Thurgood Marshall College Honors Program is minimally structured. Other than the Tuesday seminar, it offers its students very little. Within the California system, it stands in sharp contrast to the excellent program at Riverside, raising questions about the commitment of the college administration at San Diego to its own honors program. Its lack of depth may well be the consequence of the fragmentation of UCSD into five colleges, or it may reflect the profound budget crisis California has been going through. Whatever the reason, this honors program does not offer the advantages that make such programs the best bargains in U.S. higher education. ■

UNIVERSITY OF CALIFORNIA, SANTA BARBARA

PROGRAM:	College of Creative Studies
DIRECTOR:	Dr. William Ashby
ADMINISTRATIVE ASSISTANT:	Mrs. Patricia Breyman
ADDRESS:	College of Creative Studies UC Santa Barbara Santa Barbara, CA 93106-6110
TELEPHONE:	(805) 893-2364
TUITION (FEES):	**IN-STATE** **OUT-OF-STATE** $3,615.60 (incl.) $11,313.60 (incl.)
TOWN & CAMPUS:	Good
INTELLECTUAL SETTING:	Fair
ENTRANCE REQUIREMENTS:	Competitive/Easy
PROGRAM QUALITY:	Good
OVERALL EVALUATION:	★★

▶ UC Santa Barbara has a reputation for being a party school like few others, and when students are not partying they are said to be recovering on the Pacific Ocean beaches that define the campus. However much we would like to say that this is not the case, our best information tells us that UCSB's reputation is all too well deserved. There is little intellectual life on campus, and life in the neighboring town of Isla Verde is very much devoted to the decidedly unintellectual pursuit of fun. So why is UCSB's College of Creative Studies (CCS) included in this book?

Because CCS is a unique honors program that is worthy of attention, if for no other reason than that it stretches the definition of an honors program. It is an alternative to traditional undergraduate education. There are no more than 175 students in CCS, and they participate in classes that range in size from four to 20. Grading is done on a system of pass or no record, an ingenious method that eliminates virtually all pressure from the program. At the end of every quarter, the instructor determines the number of units each student's work merits for the course.

Admission is to the UCSB first of all, and this campus generally expects at least a 3.2 high school GPA and a score of at least 1000 on the SAT. Prospective students should know, however, that the requirements to gain admission into one of the disciplines that make up the CCS are much higher. To study physics, for example, a minimum score of 720 on the math section of the SAT is required, and there are several students studying mathematics who scored a perfect 800. The University practices rolling admissions, meaning that applicants are accepted as they apply, but there are priority mailing dates that bring some order to the system. Ask the Admissions Office about this.

CCS offers students seven areas of emphasis to choose from: art (mainly studio art), biology, chemistry, literature, mathematics, music composition, and physics. Space does not allow a description of all seven fields, so we shall describe only two—literature and music—in detail.

Students choosing literature are expected to have a passion for it. They bypass surveys and begin immediately with advanced courses that follow a traditional curriculum. Normally what is meant by literature is English, American, and foreign literature in translation. Students take small classes in Greek drama, American novels, Latin American fiction, Chinese and Japanese poetry, and the modern short story. Selected courses are offered on the works of such individual authors as Austen, Dickens, Lawrence, and Hemingway. All students are expected to complete at least one course on Chaucer, Shakespeare, and Milton. Students in the literature emphasis may also take standard literature courses offered by the English Department and other language departments. Applicants to this program are expected to submit at least one analytical essay as well as three samples of fiction and/or verse.

Students choosing music are expected to read and write standard musical notation and have a talent for composition. Here, as in literature, the curriculum is traditional. Students learn to compose music understood to be serious, or of concert hall quality. Basically, the student works with his or her advisor and aspires to complete work even in the first year. Around this nucleus is built a set of more traditional background courses on major composers, movements, and periods. Applicants for the music emphasis are expected to submit scores of original compositions and, if possible, audio recordings.

As noted, there are usually about 175 students in CCS. Of these, 40 percent are women and 2 or 3 percent are minorities. There are no

African-Americans and only a few Hispanics at present. About 6 percent of the small student body is from out of state, and this figure may decline with rising tuition.

To say the least, UCSB presents a contradictory picture. The University has a well deserved reputation as a fun-loving party school, but the College of Creative Studies appears to be a good place for highly motivated and very mature students. ■

UNIVERSITY OF CONNECTICUT

PROGRAM:	Honors Scholar Program
DIRECTOR:	Prof. Cyrus E. Zirakzadeh
ASSOCIATE DIRECTOR:	Mrs. Patricia M. Szarek
ADDRESS:	Honors Program U-147, Wood Hall, Room 113 241 Glenbrook Road Storrs, CT 06269-2147
TELEPHONE:	(203) 486-4223
TUITION (FEES):	IN-STATE: $3,476 ($814) OTHER NEW ENGLAND STATES: $5,214 ($814) OUTSIDE NEW ENGLAND: $10,596 ($814)
TOWN & CAMPUS	Fair
INTELLECTUAL SETTING:	Fair
ENTRANCE REQUIREMENTS:	Competitive
PROGRAM QUALITY:	Good
OVERALL EVALUATION:	★★

▶ Storrs is a dull town, and the university campus is also not the most inspiring place. Intellectual life is not intense, probably because of the preprofessional orientation of the undergraduates. Lecture classes in the first two years tend to be huge in this university of 23,000. Most of these students are from in-state, and since Connecticut is a small state, this means that many go home on weekends. This is not an ideal setting for an honors program.

Entrance requirements are competitive but on the easy side. The Honors Scholar Program grants automatic admission to anyone having an SAT score of at least 1200, with at least a 600 in each component, and a standing in the top 10 percent of the high school graduating class. The program will consider students who fall short of these standards, looking at what they have taken in high school and whether there is something else to recommend them.

The ideals of the Honors Scholar Program are honest but uninspired. The program itself is a different story. Freshmen and sophomores are required to take an aggregate of six honors courses in the first two years. By doing so they fulfill core requirements and avoid the mass lecture classes that give the University of Connecticut a bad name. This indicates a strongly front-loaded program, in which honors students are taking nearly one-half their underclass courses in small and demanding honors sections of 12 to 18 students, usually taught by full-time faculty. Freshmen and sophomores are required to maintain a GPA of 3.2 to remain in the program.

Students who have successfully completed 23 honors credits with an overall GPA of 3.2 are awarded a Sophomore Honors Certificate. In the fifth semester, continuing students apply for acceptance by the honors committees of their selected majors. Individual departments may have higher standards than the Honors Scholar Program, and students who complete it are not guaranteed admission to the honors programs in their major fields.

In the junior and senior years, continuing participants take at least 12 credits of honors courses in their majors, among which must be three credits in supervised study leading to a senior thesis or a comprehensive exam. If all of this is completed with an overall 3.2 GPA, they are declared eligible for the Honors Scholar designation at graduation.

The Honors Scholar Program is housed in a seventeenth-century wood frame house, but its offices are located elsewhere. Ranking high among the activities at Honors House are informal get-togethers with professors in which serious topics are systematically addressed. These so-called mini-courses strongly enrich an already rich program. Underclassmen are required to participate in one mini-course to qualify for the Sophomore Honors Certificate.

About 175 freshmen are admitted annually to the Honors Scholar Program, and the total number of students currently enrolled is about 650. Of this number, about 60 percent graduate from the University of Connecticut with the Honors Scholar designation. The program does not keep statistics on the number of women, minorities, or out-of-state participants. As yet, there is no special housing provided for honors students, but there is no problem getting dormitory space at the University of Connecticut. An air-conditioned honors dormitory is scheduled to open in 1996.

All in all, the Honors Scholar Program at the University of Connecticut is sound. Its great advantage is that it is front-loaded, thereby enabling the honors student to avoid the mass lectures characteristic of core requirements. The disadvantage is its context: the University and Storrs are simply not inspired places. ■

UNIVERSITY OF DELAWARE

PROGRAM:	University Honors Program
DIRECTOR:	Prof. Robert F. Brown
ASSOCIATE DIRECTOR (ACTING):	Prof. Kathleen M. Duke
ADDRESS:	University Honors Program University of Delaware Newark, DE 19716
TELEPHONE:	(302) 451-1128
TUITION (FEES):	**IN-STATE** $3,550 (incl.) **OUT-OF-STATE** $9,650 (incl.)
TOWN & CAMPUS:	Fair
INTELLECTUAL SETTING:	Good
ENTRANCE REQUIREMENTS:	Competitive
PROGRAM QUALITY:	Excellent
OVERALL EVALUATION:	★ ★ ★

▶ The town of Newark is small and pleasant. The University is oriented toward science and engineering, as befits an institution living in the shadow of the DuPont corporation. It is only partly supported by the state, most of its funding coming from the generosity of the DuPont corporation. The humanities are said to be weak, but officials at Delaware claim that they are much stronger than their reputation would indicate. Music is certainly outstanding at Delaware. Philadelphia and Baltimore, both very interesting cities, are within an hour's drive, and New York and Washington, D.C., are within two hours' drive.

The University Honors Programs stresses that its entrance requirements are competitive but flexible. The admissions committee insists that the academic quality of the applicant's high school experience will be taken into careful consideration, and those who have pursued rigorous studies will be given a decided advantage. Two-thirds of successful applicants in a recent year had SAT scores of 1200 or better, which of course means that one-third had below 1200. Only a few had below 1100.

The majority of the 1991 entering honors class were in the top 5 percent of their high school graduating class, and the overwhelming majority were in the top 10 percent. Their median high school GPA was 3.72, and Delaware insists that high school GPA is a more important statistic for entry than the SAT score. The cutoff seems to be 3.5; few students with a lower GPA are admitted. (Delaware calculates the high school GPA by including only academic courses and by giving no extra points for these.)

Delaware also insists that it looks carefully at trend lines in high school GPAs: a student with a low high school GPA but an upward trend line from a bad freshman year will be preferred to a student with a higher GPA but a downward trend in grades.

The Delaware honors program is decidedly front-loaded. Freshmen are required to take at least 15 credits in honors courses, which is approximately half the freshman course load. Most of these courses replace required core courses and are taken in small sections of 20 or fewer students with excellent full-time faculty (five faculty members have appointments with the honors program). At least one course in the freshman year must be an honors colloquium and another an honors forum. Some of the colloquia are interdisciplinary courses; all have an intensive writing component. The forum courses cover a wide range of topics to broaden the intellectual horizons of the student.

Freshmen are required to live in honors residences, the Dickinson Halls, which house some nonhonors students as well. The hallmark of the dormitories is a program of extracurricular activities that are designed to encourage a sense of community among the honors students. The dormitories are mentored by a small number of the previous year's freshmen, who are called Dickinson fellows.

After the freshman year, in which first-year honors certificates may be earned, honors students are under no specific obligations but have various honors options available to them. The advanced Honors Certificate calls for 21 honors credits beyond the freshman year, an intensive advising process, and a GPA of 3.0. Students seeking an honors degree must earn a total of 15 honors credits, write a senior thesis, and have a 3.4 GPA. Students seeking a degree with distinction must earn an overall GPA of 3.0 and 3.5 in their major, but need no specific number of honors credits.

The Honors Center, a building that is centrally located on campus just opposite the university library and near the President's house, is open seven days a week until midnight and provides a selection of reading rooms and lounges equipped with reference materials.

After the freshman year, honors students may choose to continue to live in honors housing, in one of Delaware's special-interest houses, including small units where foreign languages are spoken.

Normally, 255 to 300 freshmen are admitted annually to the program, which currently has a total of 1,000 students, 90 percent of whom graduate from the university. Of this total, 52 percent are women and 14 percent are minorities. Sixteen of the 292 students admitted for 1992 were African-Americans, one was Hispanic, and 22 were Asian-Americans. Because Delaware is a small state, a large proportion of students—more than two-thirds—come from out of state, from nearby Maryland, New Jersey, and Pennsylvania.

In sum, the Delaware program is excellent, even outstanding. Newark is not Austin or Amherst, but for all that, this is one of the best programs in the United States, and for its quality it is relatively easy to get into. ■

UNIVERSITY OF FLORIDA

PROGRAM:	The Honors Program
DIRECTOR:	Prof. Keith Legg
ASSOCIATE DIRECTOR:	Prof. John Reiskind
ADDRESS:	Honors Program Office 352 Little Hall University of Florida Gainesville, FL 32611
TELEPHONE:	(904) 392-1519
TUITION (FEES):	**IN-STATE** $1,350 (incl.) **OUT-OF-STATE** $5,280 (incl.)
TOWN & CAMPUS:	Fair
INTELLECTUAL SETTING:	Fair
ENTRANCE REQUIREMENTS:	Very Competitive
PROGRAM QUALITY:	Good
OVERALL EVALUATION:	★★

▶ The University of Florida in Gainesville, with 35,000 students, is perhaps the largest and most modern southern university. It is a party school by night and an education factory by day. Intellectual life and atmosphere are fair, not good. Fraternities are everywhere, and there is a serious dormitory shortage that sends students into Gainesville seeking apartments.

Entrance requirements to the Honors Program are very competitive. Florida expects a minimum 3.6 high school GPA (which they weight for Advanced Placement or other demanding high school courses), as well as a 1280 on the SAT or a composite score of 30 on the ACT. Asked whether they were flexible on these standards, officials at the Honors Program replied that only rare exceptions are made, and these usually for students with higher GPAs and lower SATs. The program is able to maintain its high standard because it attracts a large number of National Merit Scholars, National Achievement Scholars, and National Hispanic Scholars by offering generous scholarships.

UNIVERSITY OF FLORIDA

The Honors Program requires that students take at least one honors course in each of their first four semesters, and it provides two kinds of courses: honors sections of regular courses and special courses designed for the Honors Program. These courses are taught by full-time professors in seminar style and have no more than 22 students, often fewer. Given the large scale of Florida's introductory lecture courses, it pays to take more than one honors section per term in the first two years. If one maintains a 3.0 GPA, one is given an honors certificate at the end of the first two years.

Thereafter a student may shift gears and take honors courses at one of the many colleges at the University of Florida, doing departmental honors in the upperclass years. Since there are so many majors, it is impossible to describe what this entails, but it must be noted that these programs are entirely separate from the Honors Program.

Most significantly, the University of Florida's Honors Program is entirely front-loaded. In fact, it is unusual if not unique in that one completes the Honors Program at the end of four terms, or with 60 credits. We therefore directed our questions to the type of courses and advisement available in the first four terms. Might one, for example, take two honors seminars per term for the first four terms and complete the university's general education (core) requirements without ever taking a large lecture? The answer is yes. In fact, students average 1.5 honors courses per term for the first four terms, taking a total of six courses, or 18 credits on average. Sixty honors sections are offered per term, thereby providing 1,320 places to the students in the program, or approximately 1.5 courses per term per student.

Housing is a problem at the University of Florida, but not for students in the Honors Program. Two renovated dormitories, East and Weaver Halls, are at the program's disposal, and they provide accommodation for more than 400 honors students, about 75 percent of whom are freshmen. All women are guaranteed dormitory places. Other than in these two halls, the Honors Program sees to it that its students are given space in other dormitories.

Tuition at the University of Florida is reasonable. In-state students pay $54 per credit, which if we assume a 24-credit annual load, comes out to $1,296 a year (less fees). Out-of-state students pay $213 per credit, or $5,112 annually (less fees).

There are currently 934 students in the Florida Honors Program. Of these, 50 percent are freshmen, 50 percent are sophomores, 40 percent are women, 15 percent are minorities, and 12 percent are from out of state, about one-half of these from neighboring southern states. We were concerned with the breakdown of minorities, and learned that of the 74 minority admissions this year, 35 were Asian-Americans, 14 were African-American, and 25 were Hispanic.

There are shortcomings to the University of Florida, but there are few drawbacks to the Honors Program. It has very high quality students and is totally front-loaded, which seems to us to be a good combination. ■

UNIVERSITY OF GEORGIA

PROGRAM:	The Honors Program
DIRECTOR:	Dr. Lothar L. Tresp
ASSOCIATE DIRECTOR:	Dr. Joy P. Williams
ADDRESS:	Honors Program 307 Academic Building Athens, GA 30602
TELEPHONE:	(706) 542-3240
TUITION (FEES):	**IN-STATE** $2,250 ($115) **OUT-OF-STATE** $5,940 ($115)
TOWN & CAMPUS:	Good
INTELLECTUAL SETTING:	Good
ENTRANCE REQUIREMENTS:	Competitive
PROGRAM QUALITY:	Excellent
OVERALL EVALUATION:	★ ★ ★

▶ The University of Georgia at Athens (UGA) is one of America's oldest state universities, chartered in 1785. With about 30,000 students, the campus retains an antebellum flavor, but the twentieth century intrudes in the form of a powerful football team and strong science and engineering departments. Although Athens is no Madison or Berkeley, the campus does have a good extracurricular intellectual life.

The Honors Program at UGA is large and strong, as indicated by its high entrance requirements. A minimum SAT score of 1200 (or an ACT score of 30) is expected, as well as a cumulative high school GPA of close to A, or 3.80. The factor given the greatest weight is the high school GPA, and the SAT (or ACT score) is seen as an important but secondary piece of information. UGA is especially interested in the verbal score, and expects a minimum of 550 in an SAT of around 1200. The average SAT score in the fall of 1992 was 1306, however, so an applicant with a lower than average score had better have an outstanding high school GPA.

There are no further admissions requirements; however, College Advanced Placement courses and scores are given additional weight in the admissions process. When asked what kind of students UGA is seeking, the answer was "bright" students, with no further qualification.

For students who do not make it in on the first try, UGA has a fairly well defined program of lateral entry. A student with a minimum score of 1100 on the SAT can enroll at UGA, and if he or she earns straight As in the first quarter (15 hours at 4.0), then admission is granted. If the initial SAT is 1150, then the first quarter GPA need only be 3.67, which is about an A− average. Or if a student has an SAT of 1100 and does not make the required 4.0 GPA after one quarter, a GPA of 3.67 after two quarters will do the trick.

The UGA Honors Program is not tightly structured, and as is often the case when an apparent structure is missing, close faculty advising of students replaces it. UGA begins with a two-day summer orientation for freshmen, which includes academic advising and early registration. Two weeks at the beginning of each quarter are used to give students intense advising. This is done by faculty members who have had a long association with the program. Honors Program students are given priority in the registration process.

Students are asked to take at least one honors course per quarter, and this is not difficult since the UGA Honors Program offers about 65 honors sections (courses) per quarter, many in multiple sections. The average number of students per section is 15 to 25, and the faculty is among the best that the university has to offer. Many of the sections satisfy core requirements, or, put differently, every core requirement at UGA has a corresponding honors section, so the ambitious student can skip many of the huge lecture courses for which state universities are notorious.

For example, the Honors Science Sequence, a year-long course, introduces the basic concepts of physics, chemistry, geology, and biology in an integrated fashion. The Honors Field Geology Program is open to students from all majors. It takes groups of participants to the western part of the United States to study geology in such places as the Grand Canyon. Only 20 students are taken annually. They earn 10 hours of credit in introductory geology and five hours of credit in anthropology, which also satisfies the university's environmental literacy requirement. Quite a few of the students who enter UGA as undecided end up being geology majors as a result of this program.

Another feature that gives students the opportunity to use the great variety of university resources is the Area Study Major, which allows honors students to design their own major programs using courses from different departments, resulting in truly interdisciplinary study. In recent years, one student graduated with a major in science/ethics and another in environmental management.

Back in the mainstream, honors students choose from the 65 offered honors sections not only at the freshman level but all the way up to graduate seminars. So-called senior division courses parallel regular electives but have small class sizes and are more sophisticated. Special problems seminars are offered, as are regular courses with an honors option, which entails working more closely with the professor on extra assignments. Honors students must maintain an overall GPA of 3.3 to remain in the program.

The UGA Honors Program is large, with approximately 1,000 students in all. This year, 340 new freshmen were admitted to the program. Of the total number of students, 50 percent were women and nearly 10 percent were minorities, the latter including Hispanics and Asian-Americans. The number of African-Americans in the program was about 5 percent of the total, lower than the number of African-Americans in the state and in the university as a whole. About 10 percent of honors students are from out of state, and while most of these are from neighboring states, it is interesting to note that more than a few are from more distant areas, such as Virginia and New England. This is something of a tribute to the quality of UGA's Honors Program.

Special housing for honors students is not provided at UGA. Only about 6,000 of UGA's students live on campus, the rest living in private housing in Athens. Apartments there are said to be inexpensive and plentiful, and public transportation in Athens is free to UGA students.

Perhaps most significantly, while financial aid is generally available, we learned that there are special opportunities for honors students. At present, UGA offers "Foundation" scholarships according to a formula: Students with an SAT score of at least 1200 and a high school GPA of at least 3.5 as computed by the Admissions Office are given a 50 percent discount on tuition, and students with at least a 1300 SAT and a high school GPA of at least 3.5 are given a 100 percent discount. This means that virtually all students in the UGA Honors Program are on scholarship, and many of them pay no tuition at all.

On balance, the Honors Program at the University of Georgia at Athens is very good. It might even be better than it appears to be, but a great deal is left to chance with the advisement program. As we made clear in the introduction to this book, we prefer honors programs that are explicitly structured in the first two years because they offer the greatest benefits from small sections taught by full-time faculty during this time. Fortunately, UGA seems to have a good advisement program, so it is probably a good bet.

When context is factored in, the Georgia program still does well, although, as we noted above, the city of Athens is less than ideal. When one adds to this the financial consideration, however, the University of Georgia Honors Program turns out to be one of the best opportunities in the United States. ∎

UNIVERSITY OF HAWAII, MANOA

PROGRAM:	The Selected Studies Program The Honors Program
DIRECTOR:	Dr. Judson Ihrig
ADDRESS:	Undergraduate Honors Programs University of Hawaii 2425 Campus Road Honolulu, HI 96822
TELEPHONE:	(808) 956-8391
TUITION (FEES):	IN-STATE OUT-OF-STATE $1460 ($48.70) $4,460 ($48.70)
TOWN & CAMPUS:	Fair
INTELLECTUAL SETTING:	Fair
ENTRANCE REQUIREMENTS:	Easy
PROGRAM QUALITY:	Good
OVERALL EVALUATION:	★

▶ Manoa, where the University of Hawaii, Manoa (UH), is located, is a suburb of Honolulu, Hawaii's largest city, so for obvious reasons the university is mainly a commuter school. It is only a brief drive from Waikiki Beach, and the campus itself is attractive and seems friendly. Pacific Studies and Marine Biology are two of the distinctive majors that take advantage of UH's location. Intellectual life is not great but it is also not as bad as one might suspect given the attractive location of UH.

Honors at UH is divided into two parts, the Selected Studies Program for freshmen and sophomores, and the Honors Program proper for juniors and seniors.

Entrance requirements to the UH Selected Studies Program are not stringent. Desired are an SAT score of at least 1100, with neither component score lower than 500, a high school GPA of at least 3.0, or a B-average. The authorities at Hawaii state, however, that they are suspicious of mechanical formulae and invite high school seniors who do not meet the above criteria to get their counselors to recommend them.

The Selected Studies Program itself is consciously front-loaded, necessarily so insofar as it is for freshmen and sophomores. Students are urged to take at least two "A-Sections," UH's name for honors courses, per semester for the first four semesters. An A-Section is a small class limited to 25 students and taught by full-time faculty. Because UH has a large core program, students in the Selected Studies Program can substitute A-Sections for core requirements and get out of a good number of large lecture sections with up to 300 students.

Further emphasizing the fact that the Selected Studies Program is front-loaded, UH awards a certificate for Sophomore Honors to those Selected Studies students who have taken at least 28 credits of A-Sections and attained a GPA of at least 3.5 therein *and* overall. This designation becomes a permanent part of the student's transcript.

Students who successfully complete the Selected Studies Program may be invited to participate in the Honors Program in their last two years. Juniors take a pass/fail colloquium for two semesters, and seniors write a six-credit thesis on a topic falling within the scope of their major. Honors students also take other special courses within their majors.

Students who successfully complete the Honors Program graduate with "Honors," "High Honors," or "Highest Honors." The designation goes on the transcript and appears on the diploma.

There are 320 to 340 students participating in the Selected Studies Program and about 50 to 60 in the Honors Program. Of these, 60 to 70 percent are women, due to the tendency of East Asian families to invest heavily in male education, sending their sons back to Asia while keeping their daughters home in Hawaii. There are only a few African-Americans, for the most part the sons or daughters of military families. Roughly 55 percent of undergraduates on campus are from East Asian families, somewhat above their percentage in Hawaii's overall population.

"Out-of-state students" is an unusual category at UH. There are no contiguous states, so out-of-state students travel long distances and are likely to differ culturally from in-state students, who are usually commuters from the Honolulu area, as noted above. Out-of-state students make up about 10 percent of the total number of students in both honors programs, and these come from west coast states, specifically California, Oregon, and Washington.

Housing is a problem at the University of Hawaii. There is no honors housing or special housing privileges for honors students. Only about 15 percent of all students at the University of Hawaii are housed in dormitories, and the university is confronted with a chronic shortage.

Scholarships are a significant factor at UH, given the high cost of living in the Honolulu area, especially transportation expenses. (But consider the low out-of-state tuition, which effectively functions as a subsidy for transportation costs.) There are no scholarships specifically assigned to honors students, and although UH scholarships are said to be competitive in general, it is a commentary on the status of the honors program that it is not given special scholarship funding.

The two honors programs discussed above strike us as well conceived. If UH has a weakness, it is its relatively low entrance requirements, for this works to undermine one of the advantages of honors programs, the stimulus offered by high quality students. A second problem is one of UH's greatest advantages, its location: There is no way to take a short trip without also taking a very long trip back to the mainland. A final drawback is the fact that this program is not strongly supported by the university administration. ■

UNIVERSITY OF IDAHO

PROGRAM:	University Honors Program
DIRECTOR:	Prof. Marvin Henberg (Philosophy)
ASSOCIATE DIRECTOR:	Prof. Daniel Zirker (Political Science)
ADDRESS:	University Honors Program University of Idaho Moscow, ID 83843
TELEPHONE:	(512) 471-1442
TUITION (FEES):	IN-STATE OUT-OF-STATE None ($1,426) $3,900 ($1,426)
TOWN & CAMPUS:	Fair
INTELLECTUAL SETTING:	Fair
ENTRANCE REQUIREMENTS:	Competitive
PROGRAM QUALITY:	Good
OVERALL EVALUATION:	★ ★

▶ With only 9,000 students, the University of Idaho is one of the smaller state universities in the United States. It is dominated by its engineering facilities as well as the traditional agricultural departments, and its location in Moscow, Idaho, reflects this. Moscow is a small city surrounded by wheat fields and dominated by a farming spirit. It is located seven miles from Pullman, Washington, home of Washington State University, and is about 90 miles away from Spokane.

The University Honors Program is entry-level and university-wide. In 1991, 49 percent of the honors students majored in liberal arts, 25 percent in engineering, and the remainder in agriculture and other fields, so it is fair to say that the program runs against the engineering grain of the university.

Entrance requirements are competitive but flexible. Applicants are expected to have scored a minimum of 28 on the ACT or 1200 on the SAT, *or* have a high school GPA of at least 3.7. Underachievers and overachievers are welcome, meaning that only one of these standards need be met. Two essays, each of two double-spaced typed pages, must be submitted, answering questions on public policy and personal experience.

The Idaho University Honors Program requires students to take 30 of their 128 credits in honors classes, 18 in the first two years and 12 in the last two years. Students seldom take more than this, it is said, usually because of scheduling requirements in the major departments. Idaho's best majors are in engineering, but students in the Honors Program show no strong preference for any major.

Honors classes in the first two years are small, ranging from 20 to 25 students, in contrast to normal classes of 50 to 200 students. There are no designated honors faculty members; departments select instructors, and the Honors Program may complain only after the fact. The program does not have a special dormitory for honors students, although this is high on its wish list.

There are 400 students in the University Honors Program. Seventy percent of Idaho honors students are from in-state, and the ratio of men to women is 50/50. There are no statistics on minorities, but the number is very small, reflecting the relatively small number of minorities in Idaho.

The good news from the University of Idaho is that in-state students currently pay no tuition and out-of-state students pay only $3,900 annually. No information was available on scholarships, but at this price there can be no complaints.

The Idaho University Honors Program rates two stars for a number of reasons. It is good but the university is not located in a stimulating town, and a campus dominated by engineering students is not the best environment for an honors program oriented toward liberal arts. The program is also small in terms of the number of credits it requires, and we suspect that this is because a larger program would work to the disadvantage of engineering students. ■

University of Illinois, Urbana–Champaign

Program:	Campus Honors Program
Acting Director:	Prof. Bruce Michelson
Associate Director:	Ms. Sonia Carringer
Assistant Director:	Ms. Nancy Lockmiller
Assistant Director:	Ms. Kimiko Gunji
Address:	Campus Honors Program University of Illinois 1205 West Oregon Street Urbana, IL 61801
Telephone:	(217) 244-0922
Tuition (Fees):	**IN-STATE** $2,486 ($920) **OUT-OF-STATE** $6,738 ($920)
Town & Campus:	Good
Intellectual Setting:	Good
Entrance Requirements:	Very Competitive
Program Quality:	Good
Overall Evaluation:	★★

▶ The U of I, as it is often called, is a solid, high quality Big Ten university that gets less recognition than it deserves. The campus, which straddles the small cities of Champaign and Urbana, is centered upon a magnificent central mall but is otherwise a sprawl of undistinguished architecture. The university tends to be preprofessional in orientation, with many engineering, agriculture, and business students, but what gives it its high quality is the large cohort of students from the Chicago suburbs, who give the U of I a cosmopolitan atmosphere that few other Big Ten schools have.

Entrance requirements to the Campus Honors Program (CHP) are said to be very competitive. Unfortunately, the university does not specify the statistics it is looking for, except to say that ACT scores should be in the 30s and SAT scores should correspond to this (30=1240). The reason for this deliberate vagueness is a desire to retain maximum flexibility since the CHP represents all colleges and needs to foster a community diverse in interests and backgrounds. Prospective engineering students tend to submit very different numbers from prospective students from other colleges, and if CHP is to attain its policy goal of reflecting overall campus demographics, it must have different standards for different colleges.

In addition, the CHP requires a one-page essay on a specified theme. They are looking for a demonstration of thoughtfulness, clarity, organization, and verbal skills. A second and much more personal essay is also required, and here prospective students are asked to describe some aspect of themselves that is not revealed in the other application materials. Students must apply first to the university, which has an early deadline, and then to the CHP, which has a deadline of February 1. There are approximately 700 applicants for the 100 available openings.

For each of the first four semesters, students in the Campus Honors Program are expected to take at least one of the CHP offerings, which are small seminars (a maximum of 15 students) that may be used to satisfy general requirements. During each of these first four semesters, students also attend one Scholar/Adventurers Series presentation. These are lectures by Illinois faculty engaged in stimulating and interesting research. There is also a one-time-only requirement to attend a dress rehearsal/lecture at the Krannert Center, which is a complex of theaters and concert halls.

During the upperclass years, students must enroll in at least one interdisciplinary honors seminar (LAS 295). To remain in good standing in the CHP and to graduate with honors, students must maintain at least a 4.0 GPA on the 5.0 scale used at Illinois.

The above description surveys the minimal requirements of the Campus Honors Program, which amount to five courses plus attendance at five extracurricular events, a very thin program. This is due to the large number of engineering participants in the program, who have lockstep curricula that leave little room for electives.

Beyond the minimum stated requirements, the Campus Honors Program encourages students to take additional honors courses and, more significantly, provides the means to do so. In the first four semesters, a variety of small sections of basic courses are offered for honors students. Similarly, four or five interdisciplinary seminars are offered each semester during the junior and senior years. Thus, many students go beyond the five-course requirement.

Additional benefits to the CHP include $1,000 Summer Research Awards, which allow students to spend eight weeks exploring a topic under the supervision of a faculty member. Also available to CHP students are $1,000 awards for going abroad during the summer to pursue academic projects, such as participating in a parliamentary internship in London or an archeological excavation in Rome. A single $1,000 transportation award is available for a CHP student to spend two months in Yanai, Japan, where the local Rotary Club pays most expenses. Other opportunities offered by the program include privileged access to the University Library (one of the largest in the United States) as well as use of computer labs in the honors center.

No special honors housing is provided, but this reflects the desire of CHP students not to have separate housing. There is an "Honors Cluster" in one of the dorms, but this is by choice and only involves about 20 CHP students.

Out-of-state tuition at the University of Illinois is approximately $6,738 annually, but note that 15 out-of-state students accepted into the CHP are given a waiver and are expected to pay only in-state tuition, which is $2,486 for entering freshmen. This discount is renewable for a second year if the student remains in good standing in the program, but is *not* renewable beyond the second year unless the student is able to establish residency. The two-year out-of-state tuition waiver is worth about $8,500 in savings!

About 100 incoming freshmen are added to the Illinois program each year, and the total number participating in the program is usually a little more than 400. Of this, about 42 percent are women and 6 percent are underrepresented minorities. Among the minority participants are five African-American students and 18 Hispanics. Seventeen percent of program participants are out-of-state and foreign students, the majority of whom are from neighboring midwestern states. Most of the remaining out-of-state students are from eastern states.

On balance, the University of Illinois's Campus Honors Program is attractive. It offers a variety of small sections that dovetail with the university's general requirements, and it does this in a campus setting that is stimulating. Perhaps the main advantage of the Illinois CHP is the tuition waiver for out-of-state students. The downside is that its requirements are minimal, that Urbana–Champaign is not an exciting place to be, and that the CHP lacks a capstone experience in the upperclass years. ■

INDIANA UNIVERSITY

PROGRAM:	The Honors Division
DIRECTOR:	Prof. James S. Ackerman
ASSOCIATE DIRECTOR:	Prof. Julia C. Bondanella
ADDRESS:	University Honors Division Indiana University 324 North Jordan Bloomington, IN 47405
TELEPHONE:	(812) 855-3555
TUITION (FEES):	**IN-STATE** $2,582 (incl.) **OUT-OF-STATE** $8,293 (incl.)
TOWN & CAMPUS:	Good
INTELLECTUAL SETTING:	Good
ENTRANCE REQUIREMENTS:	Competitive/Easy
PROGRAM QUALITY:	Fair
OVERALL RATING:	★★

▶ The Indiana campus is unusually charming, with a woodsy, almost rustic quality that belies the fact that it has 35,000 students. It provides all the facilities and outside speakers that one would expect from a Big Ten university. Yet Indiana is also a conservative state of small towns without a large metropolis, facts that are reflected demographically in an overly homogeneous and middling student body.

In at least one respect Indiana University provides a superior setting, for it does not have a large concentration of engineering programs (they are at Purdue), putting the liberal arts more clearly in charge of the mood of the campus. The School of Music is the strongest department on campus. Bloomington is a charming small city, but it is not as exciting as, for example, Madison or Ann Arbor.

Entrance requirements for the Honors Division are competitive but flexible. Admission is automatic if you are in the top 8 percent of your high school graduating class *and* have scored a 1200 or above on the SAT or 30 or above on the ACT. If you lack one of these qualifications, you may substitute two letters of recommendation from upper-class high school teachers, one of whom must be an English teacher.

IVY LEAGUE PROGRAMS AT STATE SCHOOL PRICES

The program is especially interested in students who have taken Advanced Placement or otherwise accelerated courses in high school and have thereby demonstrated motivation. Students whose SATs are as low as 1100 and whose class standing is as low as the 20th percentile may be considered *if* they compensate for these shortcomings with some other evidence of promise.

The program is loosely structured. Entering students are encouraged to take one or two honors seminars, which are small and offered in informal settings. The core honors courses are H101 and H102, Ideas and Human Experience, and they cover the canon of great books. In addition, 40 to 50 other honors courses are offered, including courses specially designed to fulfill requirements for the Liberal Arts and Management Program, which integrates practical business training with a liberal arts education.

About one-third of this year's freshman honors class will take one of the 18 sections of H101–102 to be offered this academic year. There are about 17 students in each section, and some have as few as 15 students. There is also an array of other scheduled honors seminars that may be substituted for introductory departmental courses, so students can get exposure to a variety of possible majors.

Having completed the first two years with a minimum GPA of 3.3, students are qualified to enter the honors programs of various departments at Indiana. The Honors Division exists to coordinate these programs and serve as an advisement center. Students are encouraged to earn an honors designation on their diplomas by accumulating 18 credits in honors seminars, including at least one semester of H101–102, and by having a cumulative GPA of 3.3 at graduation.

Once again, the chief characteristic of the Indiana University Honors Division program is that it is minimally structured, with few explicit requirements. Indiana officials argue that they are able to do things this way because of a strong advisement program, and if one judges by the staff, this seems to be the case. Eighteen sections of H101–102 are offered annually, indicating that about 35 percent of the entering class are actually taking honors seminars during their first year.

There are 2,000 students registered at the Honors Division (this year's freshman honors class had 500 students). Of these, 50 percent are women, very few are minorities (perhaps 1 percent African-Americans), and about 40 percent are from out of state. Despite the high number of out-of-state students, Indiana has a very homogeneous student body, mainly for the reasons that there are no really large cities in the state and the fact that out-of-state students tend to be recruited from neighboring midwestern states similar to Indiana.

There is no special housing for honors students, but they are encouraged to live on "academic floors" in regular dormitories designated for groups of students who want a quiet atmosphere for studying.

Indiana University is not expensive; tuition for in-state students is $2,582 per year and for out-of-state students it is $8,293 per year. But this is only part of the story: The Honors Division gives more than 140 scholarships annually to entering freshmen. Indiana also offers 20 very generous Wells Scholarships yearly, and many of these go to honors students. Scholarship students must take two honors courses during their first four semesters.

Overall, Indiana University has a solid program, but it is not outstanding in any single category. The Honors Division program itself is minimal in its requirements, and although the freshman year sequence H101–102 is excellent, it is not required and not followed up in any systematic way. The campus is beautiful, the town of Bloomington can compete with most other Big Ten towns, and the intellectual setting is good. ■

UNIVERSITY OF IOWA

PROGRAM:	The Honors Program
EXECUTIVE DIRECTOR:	Dr. Sandra Berkan
DIRECTOR:	Prof. David Klemm
ADDRESS:	The Honors Program Shambough House Honors Center 219 North Clinton Street Iowa City, IA 52244
TELEPHONE:	(319) 335-3847
TUITION (FEES):	IN-STATE $2,192 ($160) OUT-OF-STATE $7,580 ($160)
TOWN & CAMPUS:	Good
INTELLECTUAL SETTING:	Good
ENTRANCE REQUIREMENTS:	Competitive
PROGRAM QUALITY:	Good
OVERALL EVALUATION:	★★

▶ The University of Iowa, with about 19,000 students, is the smallest of the public Big Ten universities. It is strongly oriented toward the liberal arts, leaving most engineering students to Iowa State University in Ames. The campus is large, with about one acre of land per student. Centered around the old state capital and bisected by the Iowa River, it is graced with beautiful buildings and wide lawns.

The university is famous for its Writers Workshop, an institution that tends to put a real edge on the liberal arts in Iowa. The setting for an honors program could hardly be better.

Entrance requirements are high and tend to be sharply defined. Admission is automatic for applicants with 29 or better on the ACT (or 1200 or better on the SAT) and a standing in the top 10 percent of their high school graduating class. For students in the top 11 to 15 percent of their graduating class or whose ACT score is 26–28 (equivalent to an SAT of 1100), two letters of recommendation and an interview are required. All National Merit Scholars are automatically admitted. The retention standard is a 3.20 GPA.

The Iowa Honors Program is back-loaded, by which we mean that requirements as well as benefits tend to be concentrated in the junior and senior years. The explanation given for this arrangement is that Iowa students tend to be less outgoing than students in more urban settings or at east coast universities and they are therefore given time to adapt in their freshman and sophomore years, so there are no required honors courses in those years. Honors sections are offered but are optional, so freshmen and sophomores can opt for the relative anonymity and less competitive atmosphere of regular course sections to fulfill core requirements.

By concentrating the program in the last two years, the Iowa Honors Program effectively becomes a departmental major honors program. There are therefore as many honors programs as there are majors on campus, so the question of what majors are good at Iowa becomes critical. Political science is said to be excellent, as is the history major and the comparative literature major. Curiously, English is not very highly recommended. Most students in the Honors Program have several majors. Popular majors are psychology, speech pathology, art and art history, and exercise science (which has a good reputation).

About 400 freshmen are admitted annually, and a smaller number of students enter laterally, resulting in a total of 1,800 students in the program. These are divided almost equally between men and women. Iowa has a strong outreach program, so about 600 of the students are from out of state, a relatively high number. About 8 percent of the students are minority, a high figure for a state that is only 3 percent minority. About 300 students graduate from the Honors Program annually.

Tuition is a low $2,192 for in-state students and $7,580 for out-of-state students annually. Room and board are $3,206 for a double room with 20 meals a week. If the cost of books is added as $600 per year, the total cost at Iowa is about $6,000 for in-state students and $11,000 for out-of-state students. This is not the least expensive state university, but even among state universities it is a bargain. As one might expect in an honors program, a large percentage of students have merit scholarships.

Among the special features of the Iowa program are research arrangements that are made for selected juniors and seniors. Qualified students are assigned to professors on research projects, working on a one-to-one basis with faculty. Qualified seniors are also eligible for an Honors Teaching Practicum, which gives them a gentle introduction to college teaching under the guidance of a senior professor.

The Iowa Honors Program is a nearly perfect example of what we mean by the term *back-loaded*. It is not very sharply defined and can easily blend into the normal undergraduate curriculum. Its special feature of having no requirements in the first two years demands initiative of students who are at an age when they are least likely to demonstrate initiative. Iowa's liberal ways might well be a sophisticated cost-management technique. The student who will be hurt by such a setup is the one who wants to be more involved but needs an extra push, which Iowa does not provide.

The strong point of Iowa's Honors Program is the Shambough House. In effect a clubhouse, it provides honors students with a place where they can come to know each other as well as faculty and staff on their own terms, cultivating peer relationships that add to the quality of life in immeasurable ways.

On balance, the Iowa program presents a superb opportunity to the motivated student who chooses to take small honors sections in the first two years. An otherwise undemanding program can thereby be converted into a first-class experience. ∎

University of Kansas

Program:	Honors Program
Director:	Prof. J. Michael Young
Assistant Director:	Ms. Sandra Wick
Address:	University of Kansas Honors Program Nunemaker Center 1506 Engel Road Lawrence, KS 66045
Telephone:	(913) 864-4225
Tuition (Fees):	**In-State** $960 (incl.) **Out-of-State** $6,000 (incl.)
Town & Campus:	Good
Intellectual Setting:	Fair
Entrance Requirements:	Competitive
Program Quality:	Fair
Overall Evaluation:	★★

▶ Located 35 miles from Kansas City, Lawrence is a remarkably interesting little city, and the campus of the University of Kansas is beautiful. Nonetheless, and despite strong efforts toward diversity, the 25,000 students at the University of Kansas are relatively homogeneous. Admission is open for Kansas residents and most of the out-of-staters come from neighboring states. The quality of instruction is said to be good, and intellectual life is what one might expect—good but not great.

The first suggestion (but not proof) of the high quality of the honors program is the entrance requirements. Kansas makes a good initial impression by saying that an SAT of 1340 or above or an ACT of 31 gains automatic admission to the program, but this is misleading; generally, an SAT of 1200 or an ACT of 28, a high school GPA of 3.5, and good letters of recommendation are required, and there is flexibility with these standards.

The honors program is minimally structured. Entering freshmen must take a one-credit introductory honors seminar with their chief advisors. This is an orientation session in which students are taught critical thinking and the rules of participating in small groups, and are introduced to their mentors. Thereafter, students are encouraged to take two honors courses per semester for the first four semesters. If they maintain a GPA of 3.25, they may remain in the program.

Juniors and seniors usually choose to make their honors courses do double duty by having them fulfill honors requirements for departmental majors. There is no senior thesis required.

The design is simple and elegant, but everything depends on the course offerings. Freshman and sophomore honors offerings are usually in introductory departmental courses, so honors students seeking a foretaste of their majors can get it in small group sessions (of about 20 instead of 60 to 70). One question we posed concerned the number of honors sections offered in place of core, or college-wide, requirements, like western civilization and English composition, because it is here that one usually gets the really big payoff for being in honors in a state university. We were told that normal western civilization courses have about 235 students, whereas honors sections have 90 students, each with discussion groups.

The difference between 90 and 235 is less significant than it seems at first glance, for there is no possibility of having a seminar format with either number. A professor trying to run a discussion is like a juggler in a circus: he or she, depending on skills, can juggle 20 or maybe 25 balls at once, but there is no professor who can juggle 90 at the same time. The more you expand the number, the less follow-up people are allowed, and without follow-up, there is no discussion.

There are a total of 950 students in the University of Kansas Honors Program. Of these, 47 percent are women, only a small number are minorities, and 12 percent are from out of state. We questioned how many were from nonneighboring states, a figure for which statistics are not kept, and were given the impressionistic answer that only a small number were, and these mainly from the Chicago area.

The facilities of the Kansas Honors Program are impressive. The program is housed in its own building, Nunemaker Center, which has a library, small seminar rooms, and staff offices. Also, some freshman honors students are selected to live on an honors floor in McCollum Hall, and there are other scholarship halls where honors students may choose to live, and they are normally given priority.

The University of Kansas is not expensive, with in-state tuition of $960 for 1992–93 and out-of-state tuition of $6,000. A number of small scholarships are offered to attract applicants.

Overall, the Kansas honors program is not a bad choice, but one must be aware that it is a minimal program with few front-loaded benefits. What makes the program worthwhile is that the university itself is sound, and although the location is not the best, it is also not that bad. ■

University of Kentucky

Program:	The Honors Program
Director:	Dr. Christine Havice
Administrative Assistant:	Ms. Mary Ann Cooper
Address:	Honors Program University of Kentucky 1153 Patterson Office Tower Lexington, KY 40506-0027
Telephone:	(606) 257-3111
Tuition (Fees):	**IN-STATE** $1,960 ($318) [15 credits] **OUT-OF-STATE** $5,880 ($318) [15 credits]
Town & Campus:	Good
Intellectual Setting:	Fair
Entrance Requirements:	Easy
Program Quality:	Good
Overall Evaluation:	★★

▶ The University of Kentucky, or the UK, is located in downtown Lexington, about 100 miles from Louisville and 200 miles from Cincinnati. The majority of students commute or live off campus, and the intellectual life is not intense. This is a small but sleepy state university, and the only thing likely to wake it up is its good basketball season. The surrounding countryside is beautiful and helps to make up for its shortcomings.

Entrance requirements to the UK Honors Program are not demanding. Applicants are asked to have a high school GPA of at least 3.5 (an A−) and a minimum score of 28 on the ACT or 1100 on the SAT. Students who do not meet one of these requirements are encouraged to make their case in writing and provide recommendations from high school teachers. They may be given "Provisional Admission," which means that with the attainment of at least a 3.0 average after the first semester, they are admitted to the program. Students actually admitted to the program have significantly higher scores: the average ACT score is 29.5, and the average SAT score is 1233.

UNIVERSITY OF KENTUCKY

The UK Honors Program is minimal and simple. Entering students are required to complete four multidisciplinary colloquia in the first two years. These are taught by 11 faculty members who have joint appointments in the Honors Program and regular academic departments. Sections have from 16 to 18 students. The colloquia are: Honors 101: The Ancient World; Honors 102: The Medieval & Renaissance Worlds; Honors 201: The Early Modern World; and Honors 201: The Contemporary World. In other words, the first two years are structured in terms of the conventional western civilization requirement. The advantage is that these sections satisfy the core requirement for humanities as well as the core requirement for English composition.

Beyond this minimal program, a number of special courses are offered for honors students. Honors 301 is a proseminar in which interdisciplinary topics are explored and a significant research paper is produced. Recent offerings by visiting honors faculty from across campus have included "The Public Understanding of Science" and "What Can We Learn From the Holocaust: Understanding Modernity in the Shadow of Auschwitz."

A number of other one-credit courses are given that offer the kind of flexibility needed to take advantage of opportunities. The Junior-Senior Network meets monthly to explore issues related to careers and to provide upper-division students with information and workshops on such vital issues as résumé preparation. Finally, honors students publish the campus literary magazine, *JAR*, which just celebrated its twentieth anniversary.

By the end of the first semester of the senior year, honors students must have completed a research project or a work of artistic expression that is carried out independently and in consultation with a faculty mentor. This is done by enrolling in a three-credit course, Honors 395, or a departmental equivalent. Alternatively, this upper-class requirement may be fulfilled by means of an undergraduate thesis, which is Honors 398, or the Gaines Fellowship thesis.

The total number of honors students at the University of Kentucky is 450, and about 160 freshmen are admitted each year. Of the total, 50 percent are women and about 6 or 7 percent are minorities. There are five African-American students in the program. Out-of-state students make up 15 percent, and they mainly come from neighboring states, primarily Ohio.

Some scholarship money is available, and, as is often the case, the best scholarships are administered by the Financial Aid office but virtually coincide with admission to the Honors Program. For example, about 20 Singletary scholarships are given out annually, which provide full tuition plus a stipend of $500. All recipients of these scholarships are automatically admitted to the Honors Program. An additional number of National Merit scholarships are given out, and then there are a large number of smaller but still significant scholarships that provide in-state tuition or lesser amounts.

Designated honors housing is provided in Boyd Hall, where 140 places are available, and Patterson Hall, which has 125 places. All of these are in demand, and they are given out on a first-come, first-served basis.

The Honors Program at the University of Kentucky is currently in a stable state, with no plans to grow or change. The present director has been in place for three years, and she has presided over a growth of about 40 percent in the program. The actual quality of the students is significantly higher than the admission requirements, which means that a very nice window of opportunity exists at the University of Kentucky. ■

LOUISIANA STATE UNIVERSITY

PROGRAM:	Honors College
DIRECTOR:	Dean Billy M. Seay
ASSOCIATE DIRECTOR:	Associate Dean James D. Hardy
ADDRESS:	LSU Honors College 201 LSU Honors Center Baton Rouge, LA 70803-5505
TELEPHONE:	(504) 388-8831
TUITION (FEES):	IN-STATE $2,760 ($100) OUT-OF-STATE $6,070 ($100)
TOWN & CAMPUS:	Good
INTELLECTUAL SETTING:	Good
ENTRANCE REQUIREMENTS:	Competitive
PROGRAM QUALITY:	Good
OVERALL EVALUATION:	★★

▶ The Louisiana State University (LSU) campus is located about one hour from New Orleans and is very attractive, with ample shade from old trees and buildings, reminiscent of Stanford University. Sports are big time, as is Greek life, and the atmosphere is definitely that of a conservative southern university. LSU is an academically sound and solid research university, especially strong in the social sciences. Given that the state of Louisiana has the liveliest grassroots political tradition in the United States, LSU is a good place to study politics.

The LSU Honors College is new as a college. Until recently it was a program, which entails a somewhat lower status in the university hierarchy. A college is normally headed by a dean, which means it has higher status as well as better access to funding. We asked what significance the new status had for honors at LSU, and were told that it gave honors a stronger presence on campus and that it was designed to make LSU a more attractive choice for prospective honors students. The LSU Honors College does not confer degrees, and is described as a coordinating college.

Entrance to the LSU Honors College is competitive but not impossible. The College would like to see a high school GPA of at least 3.0 and a composite score on the ACT of at least 28 (or 27 if you received a 30 in English), or a minimal score of 1200 on the SAT, with at least a 570 on the verbal. In addition, an essay of 400 to 600 words is required. Students must first apply for admission to LSU, and with success, qualified students become members of the Honors College as well as another degree-granting college.

The first two years of study in the Honors College involve taking several interdisciplinary courses in the humanities and liberal arts as well as honors science and honors mathematics courses. Since these courses (or their counterparts) are normally given in large sections to LSU undergraduates, there is a real advantage to being in the Honors College in the first two years.

It is worthwhile to illustrate some of the courses at the core of the LSU honors experience. Entering freshmen may choose one of two basic culture courses. Honors 1001/1003 is an interdisciplinary course in ancient civilization that meets five days a week: On Mondays, Wednesdays, and Fridays, all honors freshmen meet for lectures, and on Tuesdays and Thursdays, they break up into smaller discussion sections with one professor. The other option is Honors 1101/1103, which has a similar five-day organization but which studies the culture of five civilizations: Greek, Indian, Chinese, Japanese, and Mayan. Second-semester students take a sequence numbered 2002/2004, dealing with the culture of late Roman and Medieval European civilization.

Students who after four semesters have accumulated at least 20 honors credits, including specific courses in the humanities, liberal arts, and mathematics and the sciences, and who have done so with a 3.3 GPA, will be given the Sophomore Honors Distinction.

Upper-division honors work is intensive and is done in small sections, smaller than those available to conventional upperclassmen in a given major. These programs are based in departments, and hence it is difficult to generalize about them, but it should be noted that all departmental honors programs are under the aegis of the Honors College, so they are monitored and coordinated to meet Honors College standards. Most such departmental honors work culminates in a senior thesis.

Two honors dormitories are available to house some of the honors students: Blake Hall houses 200 women honors students, and

McVoy Hall houses 194 male honors students. Incoming freshmen interested in these dormitories should apply for this housing as soon as possible. Nonhonors housing is available and is said to be good. All but two LSU dormitories are single-sex. Honors-qualified students who are not members of the Honors College may also live in these dormitories.

There are 500 students in the LSU Honors College programs, and the 1993 freshman class totaled 250 students. Out of all honors students, about 55 percent are women, and minorities make up about 5 percent, including only 2 percent African-Americans. One reason for this low number is that Southern University, a leading African-American college, is also in Baton Rouge, and, having an honors program of its own, has a strong attraction for African-American students. LSU admits students from all 50 states, and happily the Honors College also brings in a large number of out-of-state students, 25 percent of the total, to be exact. These come from neighboring states but also from the Midwest.

As is normally the case, honors students are in a good position to compete for a wide range of scholarships offered by the university. About 75 percent of students in the Honors College are receiving scholarship aid. It is important to note that scholarship application is automatic when one submits the LSU application for admission. The university then offers an array of five levels of scholarships that provide everything from a free ride to tuition waivers.

The Louisiana State University Honors College is a strong honors program, and we are especially impressed that it is front-loaded, since it is in the first two years that honors students in state university honors programs gain the greatest advantage. The university decision to upgrade the program to a college clearly emphasizes its commitment to honors studies. Against the background of an already strong university, this is a good omen. ■

UNIVERSITY OF MARYLAND

PROGRAM:	The University Honors Program
DIRECTOR:	Dr. Jane F. Lawrence
ASSOCIATE DIRECTOR:	Dr. James J. Airozo
ASSISTANT DIRECTOR:	Ms. Kim Theobald
ADDRESS:	University Honors Program Anne Arundel Hall University of Maryland College Park, MD 20742
TELEPHONE:	(301) 405-6771 (301) 405-6773
TUITION (FEES):	**IN-STATE** $2,564 ($615) **OUT-OF-STATE** $8,168 ($615)
TOWN & CAMPUS:	Good
INTELLECTUAL SETTING:	Good
ENTRANCE REQUIREMENTS:	Very Competitive
PROGRAM QUALITY:	Excellent
OVERALL EVALUATION:	★ ★ ★

▶ The University of Maryland has 33,000 students, of whom 24,000 are undergraduates. It is located between Washington, D.C., to the south and Baltimore to the north. The latter city is charming and has two excellent museums, the Walters and the Baltimore Museum. Washington, D.C., has too many museums to mention, but at least note should be taken of the National Gallery of Art and the Smithsonian museums. The cultural offerings of this area are enormous, and the resources of the nation's capital are one of the University of Maryland's biggest attractions.

Admission to the University Honors Program (UHP) is by invitation only, meaning that students must first apply to the university and indicate on the application that they wish to be considered for the UHP. They are also required to write an essay, the details of which are described in the application.

UNIVERSITY OF MARYLAND

The average 1992 entering honors freshman ranked in the top 10 percent of his or her high school graduating class and had an SAT score of 1270. We asked what the minimum specifications were and were told that students should have at least a 3.4 high school GPA and a minimum SAT of 1250. Other factors that influence the decision are extracurricular activities, the difficulty of courses taken in high school, the application essay, and the letter of recommendation.

The UHP is simply and elegantly structured. Students are expected to take at least two honors courses per year for the first two years, or a minimum of four honors courses (or 12 credits) over the two underclass years. To earn the University Honors Citation, given after the second year, students must complete 16 or more credits of honors courses. Of these, at least nine credits must be in honors seminars, and one credit in a colloquium.

There are three types of honors courses: Honors Seminars are small classes taught by full-time faculty or outside experts from the Washington, D.C., area. They are often interdisciplinary, and usually satisfy core, or general education, requirements. Honors Versions, or H-Version courses, are simply regular courses taught in smaller sections utilizing full-time faculty and emphasizing discussion rather than lecture techniques. One-credit colloquia are small sections taught by upper-division honors students acting as TAs. Students take one of the colloquia in either their freshman or sophomore year.

After the second year, students are encouraged to do departmental honors or college honors, and most do. Programs are available in 32 departments and colleges. The administration of the Honors Program continues to function through the last two years by monitoring departmental honors and setting standards.

Perhaps the distinguishing feature of the University of Maryland's UHP is its physical setting. It has recently moved all of its operations, including some of its housing, into a renovated building called Anne Arundel Hall. Almost all honors seminars are given there, and administrative offices, the honors newsletter, a literary magazine, a computer lab, seminar rooms, a library, an art gallery, and the Honors Lounge are located there. Not only is some housing for students provided, but there is also an apartment for a visiting honors scholar-in-residence. The visiting scholar of 1993–94, by the way, was James MacGregor Burns, a well known American political scientist.

There are 1,300 students currently participating in the UHP. The entering freshman class for 1993 was 600 students, up from 375 the previous year, an increase reflecting a commitment on the part of the university to significant expansion of the UHP.

Women make up 50 percent of the current total, and fully 20 percent of honors students are minorities. Out-of-state students comprise 22 percent of the total, and although many of these are from the surrounding states, New York and New Jersey are the leading sources of out-of-state students.

Housing for 100 students is provided in Anne Arundel Hall, and additional housing for honors students is located in the adjacent Queen Anne's Hall, which currently houses 50 honors students but will eventually house 140. There are honors floors in several other university dormitories. In any case, housing on campus is guaranteed for all honors students.

Several academic scholarships, awarded on the basis of performance rather than need, are available, including the Regents, Benjamin Banneker, and Francis Scott Key scholarships. Receipt of one of these major awards guarantees admission to the UHP. We asked what was expected and were told that a prospective student would be competitive for the Regents scholarship (free ride plus) with a 1350 SAT and a 3.8 high school GPA. The Key scholarships also provide room, board, and tuition, but without some of the extra benefits offered by the Regents. Expected here is at least a 1280 SAT and a 3.5 high school GPA. Presidents scholarships are given to everyone who interviews for a Key scholarship but does not succeed in getting it. These are $1,500 annual grants. Banneker scholarships are for African-American students.

The University of Maryland provides a very attractive Honors Program. Its location is excellent, within shooting distance of Baltimore and Washington and only a few hours from Philadelphia. The coast offers many delightful diversions, and the university itself is very good, as is the UHP program itself. This one's a good bet from any point of view. ■

UNIVERSITY OF MASSACHUSETTS AT AMHERST

PROGRAM:	The Honors Program
DIRECTOR:	Dr. Linda Nolan
ASSOCIATE DIRECTOR:	Prof. Annaliese Bischoff
ASSOCIATE DIRECTOR:	Prof. Abel Ponce de Leon
ASSISTANT DIRECTOR:	Ms. Denise Pols
ADDRESS:	Honors Office 504 Goodell University of Massachusetts Amherst, MA 01003
TELEPHONE:	(413) 545-2483
TUITION (FEES):	IN-STATE: $2,052 ($3,247) OUT-OF-STATE: $8,237 ($3,247)
TOWN & CAMPUS:	Good
INTELLECTUAL SETTING:	Good
ENTRANCE REQUIREMENTS:	Competitive
PROGRAM QUALITY:	Fair
OVERALL EVALUATION:	★★

▶ The University of Massachusetts at Amherst has a beautiful, rolling campus, uglified by numerous high-rise dorms and a high-rise library. The really good news from the Connecticut River Valley, however, is the Five-College Consortium. Students at UMass may take courses at Amherst, Hampshire, Smith, or Mt. Holyoke Colleges as well as at UMass. Of course this means taking an intercampus bus, but it is well worth the effort, for the other schools are small, intimate, high quality liberal arts colleges. Amherst is a charming small town with restaurants and bookstores, and nearby Northampton and South Hadley are equally charming.

Entrance requirements at the UMass Honors Program are competitive but simple. The first thing looked at is class standing; the

UMass Honors Program wants students to be in the top 10 percent of their high school classes but will take students who are between the 10th and 15th percentile. The UMass Honors Program also wants an SAT score of at least 1200, made up of at least 600 on the verbal and 600 in math. In the absence of class standing, the UMass Honors Program will scrutinize an applicant's high school transcript to judge the quality of courses taken. Application is made to the university, and from the general pool of successful applicants, the Honors Program selects its students.

The Honors Program begins with an orientation session over the Labor Day weekend. Students are here assigned an advisor, entering a relationship that is said to be at the heart of the program. Honors courses are limited to 20 students, although often they have only half that number.

Specifically, students in The Honors Program are expected to take one honors course per term, but are given waivers if scheduling prevents them from doing this. They may take as many honors sections as they like, but absolutely must take six honors courses during their period at the university, and of these three must be at the 300 level or above (advanced). Should the student attain an overall 3.2 GPA, he or she graduates *cum laude* and attains the designation Commonwealth Scholar on his or her diploma. To graduate with a *magna cum laude* or *summa cum laude* designation, students must attain at least a 3.5 or 3.8 GPA, respectively.

At the end of the sophomore year, students transfer from the general honors program to one of two upperclass tracks: the Departmental Honors Track or the Interdisciplinary Honors Track. Here students must fulfill departmental honors requirements, and these vary from department to department. This format suggests that the UMass Honors Program is only a two-year program but this is not the case. It is a four-year program as far as advising goes, and increasingly dimensions are being added to keep students actively engaged throughout their undergraduate years. For example, a recent addition is the "Pizza & Profs" Wednesday evening lecture series. Professors talk about what it is like to be in their specific fields, and such lectures tend to be attractive to career-oriented upperclassmen.

A unique feature of the UMass Honors Program is the possibility of taking courses at any of Amherst, Smith, Mt. Holyoke, and Hampshire Colleges. Free buses run every 10 minutes daily to Amherst College and every 20 minutes to the other colleges. UMass students may not take off-campus courses in their first semester, but thereafter may take up to three per semester at different campuses, and no more than two at one campus. A certain number of seats are reserved in each course for students from other campuses, and only a small number of courses are exclusively for students from the home campus of the course. Permission of an advisor is needed, but this is mainly a means of guaranteeing that students are in good standing. More often than not, students who desire to take courses on another campus succeed in doing so. About 500 to 600 UMass students per semester take advantage of this opportunity.

Let's try to put all this into a simplified format. A student in the UMass Honors Program might well take one honors course per term for eight consecutive terms. The first four such courses would replace "GenEd" (core) requirements, thereby enabling the student to escape at least some of the large lecture sections. The last four honors courses taken would then do double duty, both by being at the 300 level or above and being part of an individual department's honors requirements. The usual honors designations would then follow from the cumulative GPA attained.

There are roughly 600 students in the Honors Program. Of these, slightly more than half are women. Statistics for minorities were unavailable but are low, with African-Americans making up about 1 percent. Out-of-state students comprise about 33 percent of the total number of students.

The Honors Program is housed in the graduate faculty building at the center of the UMass campus, and the facilities are said to be pleasant. A recent addition is a computer room with 10 PCs and 10 Macs. There is no exclusively honors dormitory, but two dormitories house about 50 percent honors students, and two others have a smaller but still considerable percentage of honors students.

The University of Massachusetts is not inexpensive. In-state students pay only $2,052 annually, plus fees of $3,247. Out-of-state students are hit with a bill of $8,237 for tuition and $3,247 for fees. The Admissions Office quotes a figure of nearly $16,000 for the total annual cost for out-of-state students. This figure puts UMass near the top of the list in terms of cost among state universities, second only to the University of Michigan.

Aside from its cost, the Honors Program at the University of Massachusetts is attractive. The program itself could be better, but it is good enough. Its greatest advantage, however, is the location of

IVY LEAGUE PROGRAMS AT STATE SCHOOL PRICES

Amherst in the Connecticut Valley: Nowhere in the United States is there such a concentration of quality colleges in such an exquisite rural setting, and through the Five-College Program, courses at these other colleges are accessible and they are the equivalent of honors courses. This arrangement makes intellectual life stimulating as well as fun. ■

Miami University

Program:	The Honors Program
Director:	Dr. Richard Nault
Associate Director:	Prof. Richard Taylor
Address:	The Honors Program Miami University Oxford, OH 45056
Telephone:	(513) 529-3399
Tuition (Fees):	**In-State** $2,149 (incl.) **Out-of-State** $9,170 (incl.)
Town & Campus:	Good
Intellectual Setting:	Good
Entrance Requirements:	Competitive
Program Quality:	Fair
Overall Evaluation:	★★

▶ Miami University of Ohio is one of the few state universities that exist in the shadow of the flagship university (Ohio State) but are arguably as good or better in quality. The charming town of Oxford has 12,000 occupants and lies near the Indiana border, about 35 miles from Cincinnati. It is sleepy and does not offer what small cities like Austin or Ann Arbor provide for their state universities. The campus is beautiful, and its 15,000 students outnumber the population of the town. Miami University provides one of the better small-scale opportunities to be found in this book. As might be expected, campus intellectual life cannot compare with what's happening in Columbus, but this is the price one pays for smallness.

Miami University attracts good students by virtue of its charm, and it has a very good reputation throughout the Midwest, although it is unknown in the East and West. Consequently, its entrance requirements are high, and most of its students are regional. The university Honors Program expects a standing in the top 5 percent of one's high school graduating class and a score of 1200 in the SAT or 30 on the ACT. Being relatively unknown, the Miami University Honors Program does not meet its quota of incoming freshman honors students, and hence it recruits from the general freshman class at orientation. This indicates that Miami is a sleeper: a high-quality but little-known program and a good bet for the right person.

But you do have to be the right person. First of all, you have to like small-town Ohio atmosphere and a campus of politically conservative students, often young Republicans who tend, overwhelmingly, to major in business administration. The families of the students generally have high incomes, and the student body is predominantly white. The university is concerned to attract more minorities and working-class students but has a difficult time because of the small-town atmosphere and relative affluence of the student body. If this is what you want, then you'll get a good education at Miami University, for the liberal arts are strong and the nation's future managers are being given a good foundation.

The program itself is back-loaded. Senior-year requirements are four honors seminars and a thesis, which is worth three credits. Other than this there are no hard-and-fast rules. About 40 honors seminars per year are offered, and those that are freshman seminars may be used to fulfill university, or core, requirements. Freshmen are encouraged to take two honors seminars, the so-called 180 seminars, and if they complete the year with at least a 3.2 GPA, they are given the distinction "Freshman Honors." Once again, this is not required.

There are about 800 students in the honors program, and last year's freshman class was 230 strong. Of these, 50 percent are women, 5 percent are minorities, and 25 percent come from out of state. All freshmen live in dormitories, and honors students entering their second year are encouraged to live in an honors dormitory, Bishop Hall.

Miami University is relatively inexpensive as state universities go. Ohio students pay $2,149 yearly, and out-of-state students pay $9,170. Considering what one is getting for the money, it is a good deal, but in terms of cost, it is still a notch above the others.

Overall, this is one of the more attractive programs in the book, *if* one fits within its cultural parameters. The program itself is not great, but there are few campuses in this book that offer the advantages of Haverford or Grinnell, and Miami University is one of them. ■

UNIVERSITY OF MICHIGAN, ANN ARBOR

PROGRAM:	The Honors Program
DIRECTOR:	Dr. Ruth Scodel
ASSOCIATE DIRECTOR:	Mrs. Lina Wallin
ASSISTANT DIRECTOR:	Ms. Linda Hicks
ADDRESS:	The Honors Program 1210 Angell Hall Ann Arbor, MI 48109
TELEPHONE:	(313) 764-6274
TUITION (FEES)*:	**IN-STATE** $4,704 ($87) **OUT-OF-STATE** $14,670 ($87) * These tuition rates apply for underclass students. Tuition is higher for upperclass students.
TOWN & CAMPUS:	Excellent
INTELLECTUAL SETTING:	Excellent
ENTRANCE REQUIREMENTS:	Very Competitive
PROGRAM QUALITY:	Excellent
OVERALL EVALUATION:	★ ★ ★

▶ The University (36,000 students) and the town of Ann Arbor exist cheek by jowl, and anything said about the one pretty well goes for the other. The university campus is tastefully beautiful, and the town of Ann Arbor is filled with shops, restaurants, booksellers, and one of America's few arcaded streets. The intellectual life on campus is superb, and the overall student body is just about the best that one will find at a state university in the United States. Arguably this is very close to being the best context for a public honors program in the nation.

Because the Honors Program has flexible admissions procedures, it does not have fixed requirements. The typical student admitted has at least a 3.7 high school GPA and a minimum 1300 SAT score, the equivalent of 31 on the ACT. Aspirants are encouraged to seek an interview. No special honors program essay is required, but the regular admissions essay is important, as are letters from high school teachers. An academically rigorous high school program is essential.

Admission is a two-tiered process. Initially students apply for general admission to the College of Literature, Science, and the Arts. Highly qualified applicants who are accepted will then be invited after screening by the Honors Program. The large number of students and the complexity of this process indicate that it would be a very good idea to be interviewed.

About 450 students are accepted yearly, and the total number of students in the program is 1,350. These are divided equally along gender lines, and about 20 percent are minorities, of which the overwhelming majority are Asian-Americans.

The program is both front-loaded and back-loaded, meaning that there are requirements for each of the four years. Underclass students are expected to take at least two honors courses per semester for four semesters, filling in the rest of their programs with two to three nonhonors courses per semester. Students may take more than two honors courses in a semester, but they are discouraged from doing this if it leads to choosing other nonhonors courses that are easy.

In the first semester, students choose either Classical Civilization 101 (honors section) *or* Great Books 191 (all sections of which are honors sections), following up with Classical Civilization 102 *or* Great Books 192 in the second semester. Although these are requirements, there are a number of options for the second semester that are published in the *Honors Newsletter*. Underclass students are also expected to carry between 14 and 18 credits per semester.

Upperclass students who wish to stay in the program must either be admitted to a departmental honors concentration program *or* be approved for an Honors Individual Concentration Plan (ICP), which has to be approved by the Honors Academic Board. Students opting for the departmental track in effect become "honors concentrators" and place themselves under the supervision of individual departments, their honors programs will be shared with regular students who have done well and thereby qualified for the departmental program. Students opting for ICP are in effect putting together an interdisciplinary upperclass program, and they continue under the aegis of the Honors Program.

Finally, in the senior year students must write a senior thesis, unless they are majoring in one of the rare departments (e.g., mathematics) that does not require a thesis. The thesis is written under the supervision of three faculty members. Seven faculty counselors provide the core of counseling service in the Honors Program, backed up by the Director and the staff, who also counsel. The retention standard is a 3.0 GPA and the standard for graduation is a 3.0 GPA along with a faculty committee recommendation.

The only bad news is the cost of the program: In-state students pay more than most out-of-state students do at other state universities, and out-of-state students pay close to Ivy League rates. For in-state underclassmen, tuition is $2,352 per semester and for in-state upperclass students, it rises to $2,592. Out-of-state underclassmen pay $7,335 per term and upperclass students $8,021 per term. In effect, tuition is between $15,000 and $16,000 per year for out-of-state students and just over $5,000 for Michigan residents.

It should be remembered, however, that Michigan charges the highest out-of-state tuition rate of any state university because people are willing to pay this to attend. Amazingly, 51 percent of the students in the Honors Program in 1992–93 were out-of-state students. The high tuition is an indirect tribute to the quality of the university. There is a good deal of scholarship aid available, so qualified students from families with moderate incomes should not be deterred by tuition rates from applying.

The Honors Program does not have a separate dormitory, but it does have separate residential units within two residence halls on the central campus. These residence halls are unquestionably good places to live.

On balance this is an excellent program. Its overwhelming strength is the university itself in its Ann Arbor setting. The only major disadvantage at Michigan is the price, but this is mitigated by the considerable financial aid available to applicants. ∎

MICHIGAN STATE UNIVERSITY

PROGRAM:	The Honors College
DIRECTOR:	Dr. Donald Lammers
ASSOCIATE DIRECTOR:	Dr. Scott Vaughn
ADDRESS:	The Honors College Eustace Hall Michigan State University East Lansing, MI 48824-1041
TELEPHONE:	(517) 355-2326
TUITION (FEES):	IN-STATE OUT-OF-STATE $4,295 (incl.) $10,655 (incl.)
TOWN & CAMPUS:	Good
INTELLECTUAL SETTING:	Good
ENTRANCE REQUIREMENTS:	Very Competitive
PROGRAM QUALITY:	Good
OVERALL EVALUATION:	★★

▶ Michigan State University (MSU) in East Lansing is the closest thing to a state university in the State of Michigan for one simple reason: the University of Michigan (UM) in Ann Arbor receives only 12 percent of its funding from the state and hence, arguably, is closer to being a private university than a public one. MSU receives about 40 percent of its funding from the state and therefore considers itself more oriented toward serving Michigan students.

MSU exists in the shadow of UM, and for good reasons. UM is one of America's greatest universities. Compared with most other flagship state universities, however, MSU easily holds its own. It has strong programs in the natural sciences and engineering, and its James Madison College, which is oriented to the social sciences, is very good. The campus is beautiful, and the city of East Lansing is a fine place to live. Intellectual life on campus is good.

For undergraduates, however, life at MSU can be trying. Introductory lecture sections are huge, required courses are often not available, and professors are relatively inaccessible. For these reasons and others, the Honors College is especially desirable if one is contemplating going to MSU.

Entrance requirements are very competitive for high school seniors. Automatically admitted are students who rank in the top 5 percent of their high school classes *and* who have an SAT score of at least 1300 or an ACT composite score of at least 30. A student not meeting these criteria may still be admitted, but letters of recommendation are needed, as is a personal statement in support of the application. Not many such students are admitted, however, for MSU tends to believe that there are problems underlying the profile of a student who is an underachiever (getting a high SAT score and a low GPA) or an overachiever (doing well in high school but not as well on tests). The average SAT score of students in last year's entering class was around 1300, and the average class standing was in the 96th or 97th percentile.

The MSU Honors College is only minimally structured. Students are required to take at least eight honors-caliber courses over a four-year undergraduate career, maintain at least a 3.2 GPA throughout, and distribute honors courses appropriately between general education (core) requirements, major requirements, and electives.

What is really distinctive about the MSU program, however, is its advisement system, which is very strong and makes firm demands on its students. The student and the advisor enter into a contractual agreement on the student's education. The contract, called the Academic Progress Plan (APP), is negotiated, implying that the student is expected to be well informed about MSU's requirements and programs and about him- or herself as well. The student is expected to meet the conditions of the APP or to renegotiate its terms as he or she progresses.

Schematically, the MSU approach is as follows: Entering students work out a provisional APP for the first semester during the two-day orientation in the summer before admission to the university. Early in the fall semester a first-year plan is drawn up, which is renegotiated as the need arises. About 15 percent of students do not have majors and need more intensive advising. Students are required to meet the university's core requirements, but underclassmen may avoid large lecture sections and take small classes or even graduate classes to fulfull these requirements.

There are 875 students in the MSU Honors College, and each year 210 to 220 new freshmen are admitted. Women make up roughly

48 percent of the total and minorities 8 percent, about half of whom are African-Americans. Out-of-state students make up a surprising 35 percent of the total, and these come from eastern states as well as the neighboring states of Ohio, Indiana, and Illinois. MSU is one of the few state universities that actively seek out-of-state students, and it does so for the right reason: the diversity they bring.

MSU provides housing for honors students on honors floors at Case Hall and other dormitories. There are about 10 large housing complexes on campus, and three have pairs of honors floors for male and female students. About one-third of honors students live on these floors, and the remainder live in regular dormitory accommodations or off campus.

Financial aid is available in more than just the conventional forms. Each year, 25 freshmen are selected to become PAs, or Professorial Assistants, and they work from 8 to 10 hours weekly on research or scholarly activities. The Honors College Research Fund provides small amounts of money to Honors College students to pursue individual research. Two Gillette Fellowships of $2,000 each are given to juniors to be used to do research in the summer before the senior year.

Larger scholarships covering tuition and other expenses are also available, but none are specifically designated for honors students. Nonetheless, honors students usually compare favorably with conventional students, and it is estimated that 20 to 25 percent of entering honors freshmen win at least tuition grants.

The Honors Program at Michigan State University is as solid as you could ask for. It is weak on structure but it compensates for this in the right way by having a strong advisement program. It is relatively strong in the natural sciences and in engineering, and it is attractive because it has so many out-of-state students. East Lansing is a beautiful place, with a good intellectual life. This is a good choice. ■

UNIVERSITY OF MINNESOTA

PROGRAM:	The Honors Division
DIRECTOR:	Dr. Gordon Hirsch
ASSOCIATE DIRECTOR:	Ms. Judith Wanhala
ADDRESS:	Honors Division (CLA) University of Minnesota 115 Johnston Hall 101 Pleasant Street S.E. Minneapolis, MN 55455
TELEPHONE:	(612) 624-5522
TUITION (FEES):	IN-STATE: $3,800 (incl.) OUT-OF-STATE: $9,400 (incl.)
TOWN & CAMPUS:	Good
INTELLECTUAL SETTING:	Good
ENTRANCE REQUIREMENTS:	Easy
PROGRAM QUALITY:	Good
OVERALL EVALUATION:	★★

▶ Two significant facts about the University of Minnesota (UM) are closely related: only 10 percent of the students live in campus dormitories, and the campus is located in the Twin Cities. The first fact is a drawback: UM is a commuter school that empties out on weekends (over 50 percent of its students come from the Minneapolis/St. Paul area), which can be depressing for resident students. The second fact is positive: The Twin Cities are a great place live. St. Paul is the state capital, and Minneapolis, besides being the home of the Twins, Vikings, and Timberwolves, is a significant cultural center. The Minneapolis Orchestra is fine, and theater is also good.

The university is divided into six colleges, and this report will only look at the honors program in one of them, the College of Liberal Arts (CLA). The other colleges also have honors programs, but these tend to be preprofessional and therefore of limited interest for our purposes. The Institute of Technology Honors Program, for example, serves students with strong science and engineering interests. The College of Liberal Arts, in contrast, is by definition of broad interest and reflects this fact in the size of its honors program, which is comparatively large.

Gaining admission to the Honors Division is not especially difficult, and the standards are not precisely set. Generally, applicants are expected to have an ACT score of at least 28 or an SAT score of at least 1160. They are also expected to be in the top 10 percent of their high school graduating classes, but no specific high school GPA is required. Officials emphasize flexibility, which usually means that a sliding scale is at work, where deficiencies in one area can be compensated for by achievements in another.

Admission to the CLA Honors Division is separate from admission to the university, and students are forewarned that they must apply to both. You may submit a UM admission bid any time after October 1, and you may apply to the CLA Honors Division any time. The priority deadline for merit scholarships is February 1. If you have any specific questions, call CLA Admissions at (612) 624-4110.

The curriculum of the CLA Honors Division offers impressive opportunities. The Freshman-Sophomore Program leads to the Honors Certificate after two years if students have taken at least four honors courses and received a grade of A in at least half their total courses. Freshmen and sophomores may choose their four courses from the following:

1. *Introduction to Arts and Sciences.* An interdisciplinary smorgasbord in which a different faculty member each week introduces the various disciplines housed in CLA to sections limited to 16 freshmen.

2. *One Thousand-Level Courses.* These are introductory-level courses (UM designates undergraduate courses at levels called 1000, 3000, or 5000) offered by the Honors Division. They are topical, interdisciplinary, one-time-only courses managed by the Honors Division staff.

3. *Introductory Departmental Courses.* College departments offer introductory survey courses, conventionally designated as 101, that survey individual fields. These are taught in small sections of 15 to 20 students.

4. *Courses in Common.* Called CiC, this is an opportunity for 16 freshmen to schedule three courses that they take together. This

enhances the opportunity for discussion and community-building.

A student who completes the Freshman-Sophomore Program may opt to continue with the Junior-Senior Program. Here one must again get a grade of A in 50 percent or more of the course work, and take at least four honors courses. At this point, one is headed toward a major, and a number of other offerings are appropriate.

1. *Honors Seminars.* These are 3000-level courses on topics not considered in departmental majors, where students have the opportunity to do interdisciplinary work with students doing other majors.
2. *Advanced Honors Courses.* Continuing through a major, these are honors sections of advanced courses at the 3000 or 5000 level. Students generally choose these in their majors or related disciplines.

Within this skeletal structure, the CLA Honors Division works by means of a system of advisors who guide students through their undergraduate years. There are staff advisors, who are full-time counselors responsible for working out academic programs with CLA honors students, faculty advisors, who are faculty members devoting some of their time to advising CLA honors students, and honors peer advisors, who are other honors students trained in advising techniques and assigned primarily to freshmen on a walk-in basis.

A number of scholarships are designated for CLA honors students. Prospective freshmen must apply by February 1 of their high school senior year to be eligible for Alumni and Fesler scholarships. There are 20 Alumni scholarships of $1,000 each awarded to incoming freshmen, and there are three or four partial tuition Fesler scholarships for which incoming freshmen are eligible. Aside from these, there are a number of university-wide scholarships for which persons accepted into the honors program are especially qualified. About 33 percent of all freshmen in the CLA Honors Division are on scholarship, so the prospects for financial aid are good.

One should be aware that at UM there are very few four-year scholarships. Freshmen winning scholarships are getting them for one or two years only, and they go back to square one at the end of the award period and must reapply. There are some awards available to third- and fourth-year students, but the situation does not offer the same financial stability as scholarships that are automatically renewed each year over four years if a minimum GPA is maintained.

Housing at UM is not a problem, but there is no honors-specific housing, although there are "Scholars' Floors" open to any student who wants a quiet setting. UM is now the only university in the Big Ten not offering honors-designated housing, and it might be moving in this direction in the near future.

There are a total of 1,500 students in the CLA Honors Division. About 85 percent of honors students stick it out for four years, or, put the other way around, only about 15 percent of honors students decide to call it quits after they get their Honors Certificates at the end of the sophomore year. Roughly 65 percent of CLA honors students are women and this high number is accounted for by the relative attractiveness of liberal arts majors to women. The engineering honors program is said to tilt the other way in favor of men. About 250 to 300 new freshmen are brought in each year.

Approximately 10 percent of honors students are minorities, including Native Americans, African-Americans, Hispanics, Asian-Americans, and international students. Fewer than 1 percent of these are African-Americans. The number of out-of-state students is difficult to determine since Minnesota has an agreement with neighboring states that allows students from these states to pay in-state tuition. UM therefore has a large number of students from contiguous states, and few students from states outside the region.

The University of Minnesota is a quality institution, and its setting could hardly be better. The Honors Program is good, and so this is a place where one cannot go wrong. ■

UNIVERSITY OF MISSISSIPPI	

PROGRAM:	Honors Program
DIRECTOR:	Dr. George Everett
ADDRESS:	University of Mississippi Honors Program University, MS 38677
TELEPHONE:	(601) 232-7294
TUITION (FEES):	**IN-STATE** $2,434 (incl.) **OUT-OF-STATE** $4,394 (incl.)
TOWN & CAMPUS:	Fair
INTELLECTUAL SETTING:	Fair
ENTRANCE REQUIREMENTS:	Easy
PROGRAM QUALITY:	Fair
OVERALL EVALUATION:	★

▶ The University of Mississippi, or "Ole Miss" as it is called, is the quintessential southern university. It has plantation-type buildings, large trees, Faulkner's home nearby, and rolling farm country all around. There is not much of a town life in Oxford, and the campus is not a great intellectual center. If, however, one is interested in studying southern culture—especially history, Faulkner, Stark Young, or blues music, which originated in the nearby Delta country and is still very much alive at the grassroots level—this is the place to be. Ole Miss has the best program of southern studies in the South and attracts students from around the world for this reason.

Entrance requirements for the Honors Program are only intelligible in terms of local educational standards. Students are expected to be in the top 5 percent of their high school graduating classes. Each is expected to have an SAT score of 1100 or better (or 27 or better on the ACT). This combination tells more about Mississippi, which is a poor state, than it perhaps intends.

We asked about the actual statistics of students and were told that most were indeed from the top 5 percent of their high school classes. Moreover, the average SAT score for students in the program is 1260–1300, or 31 on the ACT. This suggests that Mississippi's honors program is more difficult to get into than its stated standards would suggest. When asked about this, Mississippi authorities explained that the standards are guidelines and that the Honors Program is willing to consider students with as low as a 25 on the ACT (1050 on the SAT) if there are compensating factors. It is solely because of this flexibility that Mississippi's Honors Program is not especially difficult to get into.

The program itself is minimally structured and not overly demanding. Freshmen must select two interdisciplinary courses, which are small sections of no more than 15 students taught by full-time faculty and focusing on the social sciences and humanities. In addition, underclassmen may select from a range of lower-division or one hundred-level honors courses that may serve as substitutes for large lecture core courses. Upperclassmen may enroll in many honors seminars and colloquia offered by individual departments. The main advantage for upperclass honors students is that they may arrange tutorials with professors, something that other students are not allowed to do.

Honors housing is available as honors floors for men and women during all four years at the university.

Annual out-of-state tuition is $4,394 and in-state tuition is $2,434, so Ole Miss is a bargain. At the moment there is a good deal of scholarship aid available, and approximately 90 percent of students in the Honors Program are receiving scholarships. Honors students have this advantage because the names of successful applicants are sent to the Office of Financial Aid.

There are a total of 250 students in the Honors Program at the University of Mississippi, and each year's freshman class has 75. Of this number, 50 percent are women and 2 percent are minorities, among whom there are *no* African-Americans. This last is a rather amazing statistic when one considers that the State of Mississippi is nearly 50 percent African-American, but it is explained—partly at least—by the fact that Mississippi has several historic black colleges toward which the overwhelming majority of African-American students gravitate. Nonetheless, the state university system is currently involved in litigation concerning continuing patterns of segregation, so this statistic may change in the future.

About 30 percent of students participating in the Mississippi Honors Program are from out of state, but most of these are from neighboring states.

On balance, the Honors Program at the University of Mississippi is an attractive option for the student who wants to study some aspect of southern culture—history, literature, or music—and can feel at home at a Deep South university. From this perspective, Mississippi would certainly rate more than one star, but outside of southern studies there is nothing outstanding about Ole Miss. ∎

UNIVERSITY OF MISSOURI

PROGRAM:	The Honors College
DIRECTOR:	Dr. Stuart B. Palansky
ASSISTANT DIRECTOR:	Dr. Paul Casey
ASSISTANT DIRECTOR:	Ms. Sue Crowley
ADDRESS:	The Honors College 211 Lowry Hall Columbia, MO 65211
TELEPHONE:	(314) 882-3893
TUITION (FEES):	IN-STATE $2,934 (incl.) OUT-OF-STATE $8,010 (incl.)
TOWN & CAMPUS:	Fair
INTELLECTUAL SETTING:	Fair
ENTRANCE REQUIREMENTS:	Easy
PROGRAM QUALITY:	Fair
OVERALL EVALUATION:	★

▶ Columbia is a small city located halfway (125 miles from each) between the state's two largest cities, St. Louis and Kansas City. Off-campus social life is therefore spent in Columbia, which has the usual array of pizza shops and bars but is not a great city. The campus is attractive, but with an overwhelmingly in-state student body and a virtual open-admissions policy, the University of Missouri is by no means an intellectual and cultural center on a par with Michigan or Wisconsin.

Admission to the Honors College is not especially difficult. High school seniors must first be admitted to the university, and then apply to the Honors College by writing or phoning the main office in Lowry Hall. Applicants are expected to have at least an 1150 SAT score, or 28 on the ACT, and to have ranked in the top 10 percent of their high school graduating classes. For students meeting one but not both of these criteria, a general essay is also required in which they are asked to describe themselves and their interests and life plans.

UNIVERSITY OF MISSOURI

The requirements of the Honors College are minimal. Previously students had to take at least two honors courses valued at four credits per year, but now even this requirement has been dropped. They must, however, maintain a cumulative overall GPA of 3.0 to remain in the program, which is essentially completed at the end of sophomore year. When asked to describe the type of students actively participating in the program, an official at Missouri said they tend to be among the more curious students, those who want to read primary materials instead of the usual textbooks and who tend to be nonconformists insofar as they are inclined to break ranks with the routines of mainstream students.

The Honors College has a strong four-semester humanities sequence that many honors students take to fulfill the university's general education requirements. Small honors sections are offered for 101GH: *The Ancient World*; 102GH: *The Middle Ages and the Renaissance*; 103GH: *The Early Modern World*; and 104GH: *The Modern World*.

In addition to this humanities sequence, which we hasten to reiterate is neither a university requirement nor an Honors College requirement, students may opt to take four different kinds of honors sections. First-semester freshmen may take *Discussion Groups* (35GH), which are one-credit courses that introduce honors students to honors work in selected themes. *Seminars* (50GH) are two- to three-credit honors sections that are more intensive. *Colloquia* (100GH) are comprised of many types of honors courses in a wide variety of subjects; *Colloquia* (200GH) are similar, but limited in enrollment to juniors and seniors. Finally, *Independent Readings* (25GH), *Independent Study* (125GH), and *Preceptorships* (150GH) provide opportunities to work in one-on-one relationships with professors. In the upperclass years students go on to departmental honors or other specialized programs in the university and are not tracked, indicating that Missouri's honors program is unquestionably front-loaded.

About 450 new freshmen are admitted to the program each year, and the total number of students in the Honors College is roughly 900. Of these, about 60 percent are women, and the reason given for this somewhat high percentage is the strong humanities slant of the program. The number of minority students is small, about 2 to 3 percent, almost all of whom are African-Americans; there are only a handful of Hispanics and Asian-Americans. Missouri attracts a large number of out-of-state students, 20 percent of the total enrollment, many of whom come from beyond the neighboring states. This may be due to the fact that the university has an excellent school of journalism, a good reason why someone from New York or Texas might want to attend.

Financially, the University of Missouri offers no special incentives for out-of-state students: Some scholarship money is available, but nothing outstanding, and only a nominal amount of it is controlled by the Honors College. Out-of-state tuition is $8,010 annually, and in-state tuition is $2,934.

An interesting housing alternative in an international house is available for 120 honors students who are paired with foreign students attending the University of Missouri. Students opting for this type of housing thus have an enhanced cultural experience and make contacts that often lead to foreign travel. All other honors students live in normal dormitories or in private housing.

On balance, the University of Missouri Honors College is front-loaded and is loosely organized in the first two years. Its humanities sequence of courses and the school of journalism are particularly strong. The downside of the program is the lack of follow-through in the last two undergraduate years, as well as the fact that the University of Missouri is not an intellectual center, even among state universities. ■

UNIVERSITY OF MONTANA

PROGRAM:	Davidson Honors College
DIRECTOR:	Dean John J. Madden
ADMINISTRATIVE ASSISTANT:	Ms. Shirley Whalen
ADDRESS:	Davidson Honors College Main Hall University of Montana Missoula, MT 59812
TELEPHONE:	(406) 243-2541
TUITION (FEES):	**IN-STATE** $2,032 (incl.) **OUT-OF-STATE** $6,008 (incl.)
TOWN & CAMPUS:	Good
INTELLECTUAL SETTING:	Fair
ENTRANCE REQUIREMENTS:	Easy
PROGRAM QUALITY:	Fair
OVERALL EVALUATION:	★★

▶ The town of Missoula is said to be charming, well planned, and mild in winter, and the university campus is beautiful. But what really makes the University of Montana attractive is the surrounding forests and the Rocky Mountains. If you love the great outdoors, this is the place to go. The university's 11,000 students tend to be footloose, and the locals are friendly. The intellectual life on campus is nothing to write home about, but how much can a reasonable person ask for?

Entrance requirements at the Davidson Honors College are relatively easy by comparison with other state universities. One of the following will get you in: ranking in the top 10 percent of your high school graduating class *or* having an ACT score of 27 *or* an SAT score of 1150. If you do not meet any one of these criteria, you may still get in, but it will take some work. You will have to show motivation, a solid high school GPA, and a track record of extracurricular participation. Underachievers beware, for the Davidson Honors Program does not look kindly on someone who has low high school grades and class standing but a high SAT.

The curriculum of the Davidson Honors College is unquestionably the most unusual in the United States. Above all, the program is structured thematically in pursuit of three goals—community, communication, and leadership—thereby suggesting that it is more interested in producing strong community leaders than well educated intellectuals. Perhaps the courses are very good, but it is a leadership rather than an honors program. Readers of this book might do well to compare it to the similar program at the University of Tennessee. Here's how it works:

Community: clusters of courses are offered around a single theme, and the same students register for two or three of these courses. They then learn to pursue questions in much greater depth by taking them from class to class, instructor to instructor. For example, one cluster deals with "communication and community," and its courses are Introduction to Public Speaking, Composition, and Introduction to the Humanities.

Communication: these are small skills courses that develop abilities in thinking, speaking, and writing. Typical courses are Calculus, Composition, and French.

Leadership: this takes the form of a senior thesis or project that should demonstrate intellectual, moral, cultural, and social leadership. One may do an internship, travel around the world and keep a journal, or even do a traditional academic project, like an extra-credit paper.

Successful completion of the program requires that students do two clusters of courses, two honors seminars, and an honors project. All of these must add up to at least seven courses, but this would be hard to pull off; more likely would be eight or nine courses. Throughout one must maintain a 3.0 GPA overall and a 3.4 GPA in one's major.

There are 300 to 350 students enrolled in the Davidson Honors College. Of these, 65 percent are women, 25 percent are minorities, and 50 percent are from out of state. The reason for the high number of women is that the program downplays science and mathematics, but now the program is shifting the emphasis and expects the number of men will rise. The high minority figure is due to Native Americans and to Asian refugees who have settled in Montana, for the most part Hmongs from Southeast Asia who have been settled by churches.

They are said to be successfully integrated. The high out-of-state figure is due to the attraction of the Rockies and to the university's excellent forestry school. Half of the out-of-state students come from the east coast.

The University of Montana is inexpensive. For in-staters, tuition is $2,032 yearly, and for out-of-staters it is $6,008. Roughly 10 percent of students in the Davidson Honors College are on full scholarship, and 50 percent are on tuition scholarship.

For the right person, the Davidson Honors College is a fantastic experience. Clearly, however, you have to want to combine intellectual life with hiking and fishing. A number of students, characterized as "transients," periodically drop out to head for Alaska and then come back a few semesters later. The University of Montana sounds like the last bastion of the American frontier spirit. ∎

UNIVERSITY OF NEVADA–RENO

PROGRAM:	Honors Program
DIRECTOR:	Dr. Frank Hartigan
ASSOC. DIR.:	Dr. Deborah Ballard-Reisch
ADDRESS:	University of Nevada–Reno Honors Program 112 Reno, NE 89507-9975
TELEPHONE:	(702) 784-1455
TUITION (FEES):	**IN-STATE** **OUT-OF-STATE** $1,700 (incl.) $4,300 (incl.)
TOWN & CAMPUS:	Good
INTELLECTUAL SETTING:	Fair
ENTRANCE REQUIREMENTS:	Easy
PROGRAM QUALITY:	Good
OVERALL EVALUATION:	★

▶ The University of Nevada–Reno (UNR) is a small state university with a diverse student body, mainly because of the large number of nontraditional students. It is near the mountains and Lake Tahoe, and skiing is less than half an hour away, as is swimming in the summer. UNR has an excellent school of mining, and its journalism school is also good, but it does not have a spectacular intellectual life.

Only 50 applicants are admitted to the honors program each year, a relatively low number, even given the small size of the university. This suggests that UNR is holding down costs by minimizing its honors program, but for the 50 who get in, this makes little difference. The normal applicant pool numbers 120, and it is said that one has a very good chance of getting in if one applies with an ACT score of at least 27 (1100 on the SAT) and a minimal high school GPA of at least 3.65. Applicants are forewarned that the average ACT score of entering students is 29 (1200 on the SAT), so the stated minimum requirement may be misleading.

The program is tightly structured. Students must take at least 30 credits of honors courses over four years and maintain a GPA of at least 3.5 to graduate with honors. Given that UNR has substantial core requirements taught in large sections, sometimes by TAs, we asked how many honors courses are required in the first two years. The answer is that students are required to take at least 12 credits of core honors courses in the first two years, and the average taken is 18 credits, or six courses.

Students must also do a senior project, which amounts to six credits and is done with an advisor. Students may also earn from one to six credits by doing extracurricular projects, such as attending concerts or theater productions and writing a paper. This option was created to encourage students to get a fuller experience of fine arts.

There are a total of 200 students in the UNR Honors Program, and 50 new freshmen are accepted each year. Of these, about 55 percent are women, and the reason given for the higher percentage of women is that they tend to have better high school GPAs, which UNR weights heavily. Minorities make up about 20 percent of the honors population, and about a quarter of these are African-Americans, half are Hispanics, and another quarter are Asian-Americans. Out-of-state students make up about 10 percent of the total, and most of these come from California and Oregon.

Some honors-designated housing is available on the UNR campus. There is an honors floor for men in Lincoln Hall, which is the oldest building on campus, that houses about 20 students, and 25 honors women live in Manzanita Hall, the name of which comes from the Nevada state flower.

One hundred percent of UNR honors students are on some type of scholarship. About 35 percent of these have Presidential Scholarships, which are for four years and pay about half of all costs. To qualify for these scholarships, students must have at least a 31 on the ACT and at least a 3.5 high school GPA.

The Honors Program at UNR comes as a pleasant surprise. The State of Nevada annually experiences its own brain drain as large numbers of its high school graduates leave to study elsewhere. In order to hold on to at least a few dozen of the better high school graduates, UNR has created a very nice honors program. It is surprising that it is not larger. ■

UNIVERSITY OF NEW HAMPSHIRE

PROGRAM:	University Honors Program
DIRECTOR:	Prof. Robert Mennel
PROGRAM ASSISTANT:	Prof. Chris Sohl
ADDRESS:	Honors Program University of New Hampshire Durham, NH 03824
TELEPHONE:	(603) 862-3928
TUITION (FEES):	**IN-STATE** $3,550 ($830) **OUT-OF-STATE** $11,180 ($830)
TOWN & CAMPUS:	Good
INTELLECTUAL SETTING:	Good
ENTRANCE REQUIREMENTS:	Easy
PROGRAM QUALITY:	Good
OVERALL EVALUATION:	★★

▶ The University of New Hampshire (UNH) is located in the small New England town of Durham, which is postcard pretty with a beautiful surrounding countryside. The White Mountains are one hour away, as is the cultural wealth of Boston. The campus, which provides for slightly more than 10,000 students, is simple and charming. The students are said to be of high quality, but this is not a big state university with a powerful intellectual life. Along with places like William & Mary, New College in South Florida, and Miami University in Ohio, UNH is the closest one can get in a state university to a small liberal arts college. That's where its advantage lies.

The standard of admission to the UNH Honors Program is not imposing. Desired is a standing in the top 10 percent of one's high school graduation class and an SAT score of 1150 or better. We asked what the average SAT score was and were told that it is close to 1150 but that the SAT score is not the most significant variable considered for admission. New Hampshire is mainly concerned that high school students have had a rigorous academic education consisting of 11 or 12 units of math, science, and language.

The program itself is not complicated in its design. To graduate with honors, students must take a minimum of four honors-designated general education courses, one of which is a freshman/sophomore seminar. Honors classes average 20 to 25 students, in contrast to the normal lecture sections of 50 to 60 students. In effect, at least four courses replace core requirements for freshmen and sophomores, signaling a front-loaded program. Needless to say, this is a minimal requirement for the underclass years.

In the upperclass years, students must fulfill the honors requirements of their majors, and although these vary, the minimum is 16 credits of honors work, four of which have to be devoted to a senior thesis. In addition, the student must maintain an overall GPA of 3.2. The New Hampshire honors program is now attempting to improve coordination between the main office and the departments so that uniform standards are maintained.

If honors students choose a major without an honors dimension, to remain in honors they must complete 24 credits of general education honors courses and earn eight credits doing a senior thesis. Alternatively, participating students may complete 28 credits of general education honors courses and do a smaller senior thesis of four credits.

There are a total of 850 students enrolled in the New Hampshire Honors Program, and this year's freshman class numbered about 220 students, with an additional 50 being admitted in the second semester. Of these, 60 percent were women and 5 percent were minorities, including two African-Americans, three Hispanics, and 25 Asian-Americans. Because New Hampshire is a small state, there were a large number of out-of-state students, about 60 percent of the total, mainly from other New England and Mid-Atlantic states.

Tuition at New Hampshire is high, $11,180 for out-of-state students and $3,550 for in-staters annually, but we were told by the Director that it is still relatively low for New England universities. Please note that the fees are also relatively high. Asked what the total package would cost for an out-of-state student, we were told it would be nearly $16,000 per year, from which we conclude that New Hampshire is an expensive state university. There are a small number of scholarships available.

There is no designated honors housing, but honors students can choose to live in what is called an "academic awareness," or theme, dormitory.

IVY LEAGUE PROGRAMS AT STATE SCHOOL PRICES

The University of New Hampshire provides a small and attractive honors program in a charming setting. For someone who wants a something less than a high-powered honors program at a big, research-oriented state university, New Hampshire is a really interesting place to consider. It is the closest thing one will find in this book to the classic model of the quality New England liberal arts college. ∎

UNIVERSITY OF NEW MEXICO

PROGRAM:	General Honors Program
DIRECTOR:	Dr. Rosalie Otero
ADMINISTRATIVE ASSISTANT:	Ms. Mimi Swanson
ADDRESS:	General Honors Program University of New Mexico Dudley Wynn Honors Center Humanities Building 114 Albuquerque, NM 87131
TELEPHONE:	(505) 277-4211
TUITION (FEES):	**IN-STATE** $1,800 (incl.) **OUT-OF-STATE** $5,250 (incl.)
TOWN & CAMPUS:	Fair
INTELLECTUAL LIFE:	Fair
ENTRANCE REQUIREMENTS:	Easy
PROGRAM QUALITY:	Fair
OVERALL EVALUATION:	★

▶ The University of New Mexico (UNM) is a mixed package. Basically, it is an average state university, which means that it is sound but not outstanding academically. A few aspects of its institutional character make it a standout, however. First, it has a really diverse student body, with a large Hispanic contingent (more than 20 percent) and a substantial Native-American student component (almost 5 percent). It also has a strong Latin American Studies program, and given its location near Mexico, travel to the places being studied in the Latin American Studies program is easy (compare this feature with the Latin American Studies program at the University of Texas). Needless to say, UNM is also a great place for anyone wanting to learn Spanish.

Admission to the program is competitive. Applicants must have scored at least 29 in the English-language ACT exam, and although this works out to be about 1200 on the SAT, we were told that only 1030 on the SAT was needed. UNM does not pay much attention to the high school GPA, and it operates according to rolling admissions, which means that it accepts students year-round. One group of freshmen are drawn from the general pool of entering freshmen at the time of orientation, and a second group is drawn from second-semester freshmen who have achieved at least a 3.2 GPA in their first semester.

The honors program is centered around interdisciplinary seminars that do not duplicate courses of regular departments but may be used to satisfy elective requirements. Honors offerings do *not* fulfill core requirements, however, and thus they do not enable one to avoid the worst aspect of state universities, which is the large lecture sections for introductory courses.

More specifically, the UNM Honors Program requires that students successfully complete 18 credits of honors courses by taking three to six hours at the 100 level, three to six hours at the 200 level, three to six hours at the 300 level, and three hours at the 400 level. Students must maintain a cumulative GPA of at least 3.2 and have done their course work in such a manner as to have secured a reasonably broad liberal arts education.

One of the highlights of the UNM Honors Program is *Conexiones*, a summer course worth nine credits run by the Spanish Department in cooperation with the General Honors Program. Students initially go through an intensive orientation session in Albuquerque and then spend several weeks on site in the Mexican state of Michoacán. There they deepen their knowledge of Spanish and do a good deal of anthropological work.

Honors courses at UNM are graded in such a way as to give students maximum incentive to excel. Students either get credit (CR) or no credit (NC), or they receive an A for the course. CR indicates B or C level work, and NC means that work was done below the C level. CR and NC grades are not included in the GPA, so taking honors courses can only improve one's GPA. This grading system is ingenious.

There are 820 students in the Honors Program at UNM, and 120 to 180 new freshmen are admitted each year. The percentage of women is unavailable. Minorities make up 24 percent of the honors student body, including 1.5 percent African-Americans.

Because UNM is in Albuquerque, it is mainly a commuter school. Less than 15 percent of the students live on campus, with a larger percentage of resident students living in apartments just outside the campus. Every dormitory has an academic floor, where a rule of silence is enforced after 8:30 every evening. In the new "Scholars' Wing" of one dormitory, about 80 honors students and Presidential Scholars are housed.

Scholarship money is available, and as is always the case, honors students are in the most competitive position to receive it. There are several small stipends designated for honors students, but the major scholarships come from those generally available to UNM students, the most significant of which is the Presidential Scholarship.

The General Honors Program at UNM is well structured, and the state in which it is located is beautiful. The university itself is somewhat laid-back and is perhaps overly oriented toward commuters, so it does not provide an ideal setting for an honors program. ■

CITY UNIVERSITY OF NEW YORK

PROGRAM:	CUNY BA/BS Program
DIRECTOR:	Prof. Michael C.T. Brooks
ADMINISTRATIVE DIRECTOR:	Ms. Elaine B. Egues
ADDRESS:	CUNY BA/BS Program Graduate Center North Suite 300 25 W. 43rd St. New York, NY 10036
TELEPHONE:	(212) 642-2905
TUITION (FEES):	IN-STATE $2,400 ($100) OUT-OF-STATE $5,040 ($100)
TOWN & CAMPUS:	Excellent
INTELLECTUAL SETTING:	Fair
ENTRANCE REQUIREMENTS:	Easy
PROGRAM QUALITY:	Fair
OVERALL EVALUATION:	★★

▶ New York City is a large sprawl but from the point of view of students coming from out of state or outside the city, everything is located on the island of Manhattan, especially in midtown and downtown. Almost all the great museums, Broadway, Off-Broadway, and Off-Off-Broadway theaters, operas, and concert halls, discos and clubs, skyscrapers, fashionable shopping areas, great restaurants, hip scenes, funky people, and quality parks are located south of 96th Street. There is no place like it in the United States or the world. This cultural scene offers one of the strongest possible arguments for considering the CUNY BA/BS Program.

With more than 200,000 students, the City University of New York (CUNY) is a system of 17 campuses located in all five boroughs of New York City. Four campuses—City, Brooklyn, Hunter, and Queens—tend to dominate the system, and by virtue of its location in central Manhattan and its new buildings, Hunter College is by popular consensus the flagship campus. Good programs can be found at other campuses as well, however. Engineering at City and the sciences at Queens are said to be very good. Political science (Government) at John Jay College and business administration at Baruch College, both of which are in midtown Manhattan, are also excellent.

Most state university flagship campuses are one-dimensional affairs, populated by legions of middle-class white students of predictable ages and political views. Not so CUNY. Puerto Rican, African-American, Chinese, Palestinian, Israeli, and Hasidic-Jewish students mix with immigrants from South and Central America, and from the successor states to the Soviet Union. Middle-class whites are always in a minority; most white students are from the working class. Most universities talk about diversity in terms so narrow as to be meaningless by CUNY's standards, so if it's human variety you're looking for, this is the place.

The university has an open admissions policy, meaning that anyone with a high school diploma can enroll. Getting into a specific college is another story, but it is still not difficult. Generally, all that is required to gain entry to a senior college is a high school GPA of 80 or above *or* an SAT score of 900 or above. Admission to the CUNY BA/BS Program is also not difficult: Students who have completed 15 credits with a GPA of 2.5 or better are qualified to apply. Two faculty recommendations are required, as is an interview. Applicants to this program must already be CUNY students.

Upon acceptance into the program, the student must choose a "home" campus, mainly for administrative purposes, where students pay their tuition and fees and take the university assessment tests in reading, writing, and mathematics. Then the student selects two faculty mentors, who assist in designing a program of studies. This, too, is usually done at the home campus.

Students must then complete the core requirements of the CUNY BA/BS Program, rather than those of a specific college. There is nothing unusual about these requirements; if anything, they are entirely conventional: two English literature courses, three humanities courses, three social sciences courses, three courses in science or mathematics, and one year of foreign language study.

Remarkably, the printed literature of the CUNY BA/BS Program is adequate on the details but omits the heart and soul of the program: the privilege of taking courses anywhere within the CUNY system. Since this can be something of a mixed blessing, students do well to understand what they are getting into.

IVY LEAGUE PROGRAMS AT STATE SCHOOL PRICES

In any given semester, it is virtually impossible to take courses on more than two campuses at once, unless one can get them scheduled on separate days. Hence, the best way to go through the CUNY BA/BS Program is to pick one campus, "cream off" the best courses in one or two semesters, and then shift to another campus to repeat the performance. One can attend two campuses at once, but the scheduling must allow for adequate travel time. By working the system with skill, one can get a remarkable education.

For example, suppose one chooses Hunter College as the home college, because of its location and generally higher quality. One spends three semesters at Hunter, gaining admission during the second semester into the CUNY BA/BS Program, completing all the core requirements, and designing with faculty mentors an academic program tailored to individual preferences and the strengths of several other campuses. One is then left with five semesters to work the system.

Let us say the goal is to become a maker of documentaries on American government. One begins by taking courses at John Jay College, where public law and government courses are unsurpassed in quality and rigor. Simultaneously, one takes filmmaking courses at Brooklyn College, which has one of the best filmmaking departments in the world. Taking two semesters at Jay and Brooklyn means spending a great deal of time on the subway, but the connections are good and the train is a safe, warm place to read, so why not?

Filmmaking is a business, so business administration courses are required, preferably from Baruch College, which has produced more CEOs than any other undergraduate college in the United States. Two semesters can be spent shuttling back and forth between Baruch and Brooklyn, and once again the subway connections are good.

At this point, one semester remains, in which a student may choose to take courses at the CUNY Graduate Center. If by this time you have developed a taste for analytic philosophy, you can take graduate courses in one of the nation's best graduate philosophy departments, or you can take art history courses in one of the best departments of its kind in the United States. Like everything else at CUNY, the quality of the Graduate Center's programs runs the gamut from first class to yawning mediocrity to being so bad they are in receivership (or should be). But that's life at CUNY, so you have to ask questions.

That's the ideal. In reality, the entrance standard of a 2.5 GPA is too low, so many students in the program are insufficiently skilled to take advantage of the opportunity to cream off the university's best courses. A majority of students lack imagination and tend to opt for conventional majors instead of creating a unique programs. Students are creatures of habit and often settle in at a home campus and take most of their courses there. They often hold part-time jobs and lack the energy to travel from campus to campus.

University housing is virtually nonexistent, so students planning to come to the university should contact its housing office to see what arrangements are available. Hunter College has a dormitory, but usually students from out of state make arrangements to live in dormitories of other universities in New York City, or they team up with others and find their own apartments. Remarkably, New York City is a relatively safe place to live if one goes about it intelligently. Living arrangements can be made there that cannot be made in a number of other American cities.

In sum, the great strength of the CUNY BA/BS Program is New York City itself and the scattered resources of a megauniversity. If you have the imagination and maturity to tailor for yourself a highly focused educational curriculum, and the stamina to endure the commuting, you can get a great education through the CUNY BA/BS Program. ■

STATE UNIVERSITY OF NEW YORK AT ALBANY	
PROGRAM:	General Education Honors Program
DIRECTOR:	Mr. Dick Collier
ADDRESS:	Honors in General Education Center for Undergraduate Education University Library B36 Albany, NY 12222
TELEPHONE:	(518) 442-3960
TUITION (FEES):	IN-STATE $1,650 ($100)　　OUT-OF-STATE $6,550 ($100)
TOWN & CAMPUS:	Fair
INTELLECTUAL SETTING:	Fair
ENTRANCE REQUIREMENTS:	Easy
PROGRAM QUALITY:	Fair
OVERALL EVALUATION:	★

▶ Albany is the state capital of New York, and it is an unusual city, very much characterized by a sense of being left out or left behind. The Governor spends most of his time in New York City, which is 100 miles down the Hudson River, and legislators tend to leave town as quickly as possible. But SUNY Albany is a permanent fixture, with its uptown concrete campus and its more charming downtown campus. It provides a solid intellectual environment for its General Education Honors Program (GEHP).

The General Education Honors Program is for the most part keyed to the lateral admission of students already attending SUNY Albany. Students with a SUNY Albany GPA of 3.25 or better may apply for admission to the program on a space-available basis. Entering freshmen who feel they can attain a 3.25 GPA may also apply for admission during their first semester, but once again this is on a space-available basis. Presidential Scholars and Frederick Douglass Scholars are invited to be in the program.

We asked for a more detailed description of the admissions process and were told that only one-third of students admitted were entering freshmen, about half of whom were Presidential Scholars or

Frederick Douglass Scholars. The remaining two-thirds are SUNY Albany students who have attained dean's list status, or a 3.25 GPA.

Students entering SUNY Albany after September 1993 must meet the following requirements to graduate with the words "Honors in General Education Program" inscribed on their transcript: They must complete a total of at least 18 honors credits, with six credits each in two of the three following fields: Humanities and the Arts, Natural Sciences, and Social Sciences. The remaining six credits must be taken in the remaining category or in one of the two following categories: Cultural and Historical Perspectives, or Human Diversity.

Basically, the GEHP is completed in the first two years. Students may then take departmental honors, and those completing both GEHP and departmental honors will have the words "University Honors Scholar" placed on their transcripts.

Tutorials are the distinctive feature of the GEHP. Honors students take courses but also meet with faculty regularly to develop and work on related individual projects. The emphasis in tutorials is on independent course work and research.

Special housing for honors students is provided, specifically a dormitory in "Indian Quad," one of several large dormitory quadrangles at SUNY Albany.

A total of 200 students participate in the GEHP at SUNY Albany, not including those doing departmental majors. Of this number, about 50 percent are women and about 15 to 20 percent are minorities. Only 1 percent come from out of state.

The SUNY Albany program is good in a number of respects. First, its 18-credit course requirement is almost entirely front-loaded, or scheduled for the first four semesters. Secondly, SUNY Albany is a high-quality university with high-quality students. But apart from these advantages, the program is relatively small for the size of the university, and it is for the most part not oriented toward entering freshmen. Its administrative setup strikes us as relatively weak: It is run by a single person, and no matter how talented he might be, it is hard to imagine him providing adequate services for all 200 honors students. ■

STATE UNIVERSITY OF NEW YORK AT BUFFALO	
Program:	The Honors Program
Director:	Prof. Clyde F. Herreid
Administrative Director:	Dr. Josephine A. Capuana
Address:	University Honors Program 214 Talbert Hall Buffalo, NY 14260-1607
Telephone:	(716) 645-3020
Tuition (Fees):	**IN-STATE** **OUT-OF-STATE** $2,650 ($213.75) $6,550 ($213.75)
Town & Campus:	Fair
Intellectual Setting:	Good
Entrance Requirements:	Very Competitive
Program Quality:	Fair
Overall Evaluation:	★ ★

▶ With 26,000 students, SUNY Buffalo is the largest of the four SUNY flagship campuses. It provides a quality education but has numerous drawbacks: a predominantly preprofessional atmosphere, a large commuting student body that leaves the campus empty on weekends, a less-than-exciting location, and long winters with lots of snow. Intellectual life on campus is not outstanding, the new campus architecture is sterile, and Buffalo is a long way from New York or Boston. But despite these drawbacks, SUNY Buffalo remains a strong educational center.

Entrance requirements into the University Honors Program are very competitive. An SAT score of 1300 or better (or an ACT score of 31) is desired, as is an unweighted cumulative high school GPA of 93 or better and standing in the top 5 percent of one's high school class. No essay is required, and there is no separate application procedure.

We asked how many entering students actually met these requirements and whether strength in one area could compensate for weakness in another. We were told that the overwhelming majority of entering students actually do meet the criteria set out above, but the admissions process is flexible and students who can provide reasons for not meeting the standards will be considered. In such a case, the student should provide a cover letter supported by letters from guidance counselors setting forth the reasons for his or her performance.

The program itself is structured, minimally front-loaded, and has an interesting option for creative and performing arts. All entering honors students must take the Honors Colloquium in the fall semester of their first year. This is a weekly discussion group addressing issues of global significance. In addition, honors students must take at least one Honors Seminar for each of their first four semesters. Ten such seminars are offered each semester, and may be used to satisfy core requirements. Students graduating with a 3.5 cumulative GPA are given the honors designation.

The option in Creative and Performing Arts was introduced to broaden the dimensions of the Honors Program, and is designed to lead to majors in art, music, dance, media study, and theater. This program is still very small, accepting only 10 students annually, and has separate minimum admission standards—1150 SAT, 90 high school GPA, and an audition or portfolio—because it is understood that a commitment to performance often takes its toll on high school grades. All students in this program are currently receiving a grant of $2,000 annually, renewable for four years.

As stated, there are no requirements for the upperclass years. It was explained that most of the students do departmental honors in their majors, but this is not required. The reason given here is that the majority of students in the program are majoring in engineering or the natural sciences and do not have much flexibility in their upperclass years.

The SUNY Buffalo Honors Program, founded in 1981, remains small; about 100 new freshmen are accepted each year, and since few transfer students are admitted, the total number of students is only 375. Of this number, about one-third are women and only 1 percent are minorities. These unusual statistics may have to do with the strong emphasis on engineering and the sciences at SUNY Buffalo. Because sports are not emphasized, SUNY Buffalo does not have much name-recognition beyond New York State, and hence there are only a few—about 1 percent—out-of-state students in the program.

The good news from Buffalo is financial: Annual out-of-state tuition is $6,550, and in-state tuition is $2,650—both reasonable—but this is only part of the story. Every honors student is given a no-strings-attached scholarship, either $1,000 annually for two years or $3,000 annually for four years (awarded to about 10 to 15 students). For this reason, SUNY Buffalo is one of the best educational bargains in the United States, especially for students from New York State.

Housing for honors students is guaranteed for their four years in residence. Honors students are clustered in Governors Residence Halls, and it is here that community takes shape at SUNY Buffalo. The Governors Residence Halls comprise four dormitories of about two hundred students each that are known as "quiet dorms."

There are other advantages to being in the SUNY Buffalo honors program: Honors students register for courses before all other students. They are mentored by and participate in evening programs with faculty members, and advising is said to be readily available to them.

All things considered, the Honors Program at SUNY Buffalo is solid but unexciting. Its distinguishing feature is its Creative and Performing Arts option, but this is still a very small program, accepting only about 10 new students each year. If one is a resident of New York State, then Honors at SUNY Buffalo is a great bargain. Students at SUNY Buffalo are very motivated and do well in and after the honors program, but this does not change the fact that it is a minimal program governed primarily by the curricular demands made upon engineering students. ■

STATE UNIVERSITY OF NEW YORK AT STONY BROOK

PROGRAM:	The Honors College
MASTER:	Prof. Elof Carlson
ADMINISTRATIVE DIRECTOR:	Mrs. Donna Di Donato
ADDRESS:	The Honors College Undergraduate Admissions SUNY Stony Brook Stony Brook, NY 11794-1901
TELEPHONE:	(516) 632-7080
TUITION (FEES):	**IN-STATE** $1,325 ($168) **OUT-OF-STATE** $6,550 ($168)
TOWN & CAMPUS:	Fair
INTELLECTUAL SETTING:	Fair
ENTRANCE REQUIREMENTS:	Competitive
PROGRAM QUALITY:	Good
OVERALL EVALUATION:	★★

▶ SUNY Stony Brook is located 50 miles east of New York City, on the north shore of Long Island. It is one of four flagship campuses of the State University of New York. Stony Brook is outstanding in the natural sciences, especially physics and allied medical fields, but is relatively weak in liberal arts and the humanities. Compared with other U.S. state universities, Stony Brook does not provide the best intellectual environment for a liberal-arts-based honors program.

Because of its strength in the natural sciences, Stony Brook has attracted many foreign students, but, curiously, very few students from out of state, and this, no doubt, is accounted for by two factors. The fact that SUNY has four rather than one flagship campus produces more confusion than clarity: people are likely to believe that there is no flagship campus. Perhaps more important is that SUNY's flagship campuses for the most part do not field division I-A sports teams, which works against national name-recognition. The significance of this for prospective applicants is that SUNY Stony Brook is especially interested in increasing its national name-recognition and strongly desires out-of-state students.

High school graduates with a cumulative GPA of 3.6 (or a 92 average) *and* an SAT score of 1200 or higher (29 on the ACT) are normally granted admission to the Honors College. Stony Brook also looks for evidence of leadership or competence in the visual, performing, or literary arts. Strong letters of recommendation giving evidence of overall competence are also helpful.

We asked about the average SAT score and high school GPA for recently admitted students and were told that it was a 1220 to 1240 SAT and a 93.5 GPA. This was surprising, for normally the actual figures fall short of the stated ideals. Until recently, the program was administered by the Admissions Office, which relied on quantitative criteria alone. Consequently, SUNY Stony Brook recruited honors students from the general pool of Stony Brook applicants without considering qualitative criteria. In the future, the Honors College wants to lay greater emphasis on qualitative criteria.

Stony Brook's Honors College has a strictly prescribed curriculum that differs from the general education requirements of the university. The program is only four years old and remains small but is expanding. It is organized around five interdisciplinary seminars open exclusively to honors students, four of which are valued at six credits, limited to 15 students, and taught by teams of faculty. The two freshman seminars examine theories of progress in the nineteenth and twentieth centuries. The sophomore seminar studies the modes of inquiry characteristic of the humanities and the fine arts. The junior seminar concentrates on science, values, and society, and the senior seminar focuses on multiculturalism and global awareness.

Students in the first two years also take a one-credit seminar that examines the artistic, intellectual, and cultural life of a research university. This seminar meets on Monday evenings and brings in faculty members who talk about their own experiences. In effect, it works like a counseling service for students oriented toward academic or research careers.

In addition to the five interdisciplinary seminars, students are required to take five honors or advanced courses related to their chosen majors and to complete a senior thesis or offer an individual performance or group project during senior year. All told, participating honors students are required to take nearly 50 credits of honors seminars and honors or advanced courses.

STATE UNIVERSITY OF NEW YORK AT STONY BROOK

There are 130 students enrolled in the Honors College at Stony Brook. Approximately 30 new freshmen are accepted each year. Of these, about 50 percent are women and 10 percent are minorities, including eight African-Americans, two Hispanics, and six Asian-Americans. Only a small percentage of students are from out of state—the number given was eight—and this is a situation that the authorities at Stony Brook would like to change. This year, 6000 honors information packages were sent to students in New York State and an additional 1,000 were sent to students in four other states.

There is special honors housing located in a renovated dormitory called Hendrix College, where 40 honors students live with 80 regular students.

Tuition at SUNY is reasonable: $6,550 for out-of-state students and $1,325 for in-state students. All entering honors students are given a scholarship of $2,000 for one year. In addition, six four-year, full-tuition scholarships are awarded.

What SUNY Binghamton is to the liberal arts, SUNY Stony Brook is to the natural sciences, and high school students who feel inclined in this direction and who are qualified for the Honors College might consider this a superb chance to get a good liberal arts and research-oriented education. ■

UNIVERSITY OF NORTH CAROLINA AT CHAPEL HILL

PROGRAM:	The Honors Program
DIRECTOR:	Associate Dean Robert C. Allen
ADMINISTRATIVE ASSISTANT:	Ms. Sue Hester
HONORS SECRETARY:	Ms. Charlotte Williams
ADDRESS:	Honors Office, CB# 3510 300 Steele Building University of North Carolina Chapel Hill, NC 27599-3510
TELEPHONE:	(919) 966-5110
TUITION (FEES):	IN-STATE OUT-OF-STATE $1,284.20 (incl.) $7,868.20 (incl.)
TOWN & CAMPUS:	Excellent
INTELLECTUAL SETTING:	Excellent
ENTRANCE REQUIREMENTS:	Competitive
PROGRAM QUALITY:	Excellent
OVERALL EVALUATION:	★ ★ ★

▶ The town and campus setting of the University of North Carolina at Chapel Hill could hardly be better; it ranks with similar settings in Berkeley, Madison, and Ann Arbor as being among the best in the United States. There are 24,000 undergraduates and graduates studying liberal arts and science (no engineering) in Chapel Hill. Widening the scope, the story becomes even better: the towns of Chapel Hill, Raleigh, and Durham—where Duke University is located—form the Research Triangle, an area similar to Rt. 128 in Massachusetts and Silicon Valley in California in that it acts as a magnet for high-technology companies. This setting is excellent.

Standards for admission to the university are high, especially for out-of-state students, and this is particularly true of the Honors Program. What North Carolina looks for is a high school GPA of at least

3.5, at least a 1250 on the SAT, and evidence that a rigorous high school curriculum has been pursued. (The average SAT score of this year's freshman honors class is 1360, and the average GPA is near 4.0.) About 175 new freshmen are accepted into the honors program each year.

There is no separate application process; honors students are chosen from the general pool of entrants. The deadline for application is January 15. About 500 letters are sent to accepted freshmen from whom the 175 honors students will be selected.

The university reports that the top 1,000 students admitted in the 1990 freshman class had an average SAT of 1334. These students are allowed to take honors sections without being in the Honors Program, thereby greatly increasing the number of sections that are offered as well as the diversity of students involved. Over 100 honors sections are taught yearly, and annually 60 to 70 students enter the program laterally after their freshman year.

The ideals governing the North Carolina Honors Program are permeability, accessibility, and inclusivity, basically all of which say the same thing: while the Honors Program has a core of full-time honors students, many other students are enriched by it. A total of 1,200 students yearly participate in the program by taking at least one honors course. These are not only the students with SATs of over 1300; any student with a cumulative GPA of 3.0 may take an honors course.

Full-time honors students are expected to complete two honors courses per year for three years, the only restriction being that freshmen take a literature honors course (numbered 29), which may be in a foreign language department as well as in the English Department. At the end of each year students are expected to have maintained an overall 3.0 GPA, and, failing this, they are dropped from the program. Most honors students take more than two honors courses per year.

The junior year is a transition period when students may elect to complete the Honors Program, to go on to do honors in their majors, or to do both. Students must have a 3.2 cumulative GPA to qualify for doing honors in their majors. Those completing the honors program (six courses) have their completion noted on their transcripts. Students also completing honors in their majors have that noted on their diplomas.

Honors sections and seminars may be used to satisfy university core, or GED, requirements, often called perspective requirements at North Carolina. These are not necessarily just small honors versions of large lecture courses; often they differ entirely from the mainstream curriculum. For example, North Carolina has funding for Seminars in the Civic Arts, taught by eminent practitioners and useful for satisfying social science requirements. Brandes Seminars are newly conceived honors courses funded by a grant that buys faculty release time to develop curricula, and they, too, provide imaginative alternatives to conventional course requirements.

The Honors Program emphasizes but does not require that its students participate in international programs. Approximately 24 students yearly, half of whom are honors students, spend a semester at the London School of Economics (LSE), and currently the Honors Program is developing new international programs in cooperation with the Universities of Melbourne and Murdoch in Australia.

As already noted, about 175 high school seniors are accepted each year for admission into the Honors Program, and there are currently approximately 800 students participating. The freshman class of 1992 was 59 percent women and about 18 percent minorities, including 14 African-Americans, two Hispanics, and 18 Asian-Americans. Out-of-state students make up 38 percent of the total, and although most of these are from neighboring southern states, a relatively large number come from outside the region, due to the university's national reputation.

Housing is good and readily available at the University of North Carolina, but there is no designated honors housing. Annual out-of-state tuition and fees are $7,868.20, and in-state tuition and fees are $1,284.20. There is some scholarship money available. The offices of the Honors Program are undistinguished, but in approximately six or seven years the program will have its own building. In keeping with the open-door policy of the program, the building will be called The Center for Undergraduate Excellence.

On balance, the Honors Program at the University of North Carolina is excellent, due mainly to its setting, which is one of the best in the United States. The program itself is strong, but is not highly structured and seems to lack the extracurricular dimension that distinguishes honors programs at other state universities. This is not a major drawback, however, and for students who do not want to be closely supervised, it is an advantage. ■

Ohio State University

Program:	The Honors Society
Director:	Dr. David Hothersoll
Associate Director:	Dr. Mabel Freedman
Address:	University Honors Center Ohio State University 220 West 12th Avenue Columbus, OH 43210-1329
Telephone:	(614) 292-3135
Tuition (Fees):	**In-State** $2,748 (incl.) **Out-of-State** $8,139 (incl.)
Town & Campus:	Fair
Intellectual Setting:	Fair
Entrance Requirements:	Competitive
Program Quality:	Good
Overall Evaluation:	★★

▶ With 54,000 students, Ohio State University is a city unto itself, and the generally conservative student body is not very impressive, with an average SAT score of 990. Most students come from small towns in Ohio and are majoring in agriculture, engineering, and education. Ohio State provides a good but by no means great setting for its honors students.

Ohio State has not one but 12 honors programs. However impressive this number might seem, it is also an indicator of the fragmentation resulting from its strong preprofessional orientation. The 12 programs correspond to the university's 12 colleges, and each has its own honors director. The University Honors Center counteracts this fragmentation by coordinating all of the university's honors efforts. We shall concentrate on only one program, that of the Colleges of Arts and Sciences, even though our statistics will often describe all 12 honors programs.

We were asked to call attention to the opportunity provided to do research in the Ohio State honors programs, which allow students to write an honors thesis and graduate with distinction. Each spring the

University Honors Center sponsors an Undergraduate Research Recognition Event in which students display the results of their research on posters at a mini-convention.

Admission to all honors programs is competitive but flexible, and is automatic for applicants in the top 10 percent of their high school graduating class who have attained a combined score of 1250 or above on the SAT (or 29 or above on the ACT). Students who do not meet these standards can gain entrance if they demonstrate other indications of potential, such as motivation or special experience. We learned that the average SAT of students in the program is 1215 (29 ACT average) and that the average student is in the top 12 percent of his or her high school graduating class.

Arts and Sciences honors students enter into contracts with their advisors. There are no specific requirements, but there is an unwritten rule that students take one honors course per quarter. Normally, they take more than one course per term, and are given priority scheduling. They usually opt to take small (30 students or under) honors sections rather than the large lecture sections available to regular students.

The honors programs together accept 850 to 900 new freshmen every year, and have a total enrollment of 3,300 to 3,400. Of these, about 600 students are in the Arts and Sciences honors program. Here, 45 percent are women, and between 4 and 5 percent are minorities, including 1 percent Hispanics, 2 percent Asian-Americans, and 2 percent from other categories. The number of African-Americans is statistically insignificant. Only 1 to 2 percent of Arts and Sciences honors students are from out of state.

Separate honors housing is provided, including three designated honors dormitories—Taylor Tower, Lincoln House, and Bradley Hall—that house more than 1,000 honors students. Although there is nothing special about the physical facilities of these dormitories, they do offer the distinct advantage of being focal points for coordinating extracurricular activities, such as the faculty dinners that bring students together with professors for informal evenings of socializing.

The annual out-of-state tuition (with fees) at Ohio State is $8,139, and in-state tuition (with fees) is $2,748. This is neither good nor bad news, but it should be noted that Ohio State is very generous with scholarship aid to students who qualify. For example, University Scholarships of $1,000 are available to students who meet the entrance requirements of the honors program and graduate in the top 3 percent of their high school classes. These scholarships are not automatically awarded, but the chances of getting one are very good because the university wants to enhance the quality of the student body by drawing in as many honors students as possible.

Ohio State is one of those universities whose honors programs are solid without being outstanding or unusual. They are for the most part unstructured and insufficiently front-loaded, but among more than 3,000 honors students, one can certainly immerse oneself in an honors subculture. The Ohio State Honors Programs are far from being the best in the nation, and with their small number of out-of-state students and minorities, they promise a culturally homogeneous experience. ■

UNIVERSITY OF OKLAHOMA

PROGRAM:	The Honors Program
DIRECTOR:	Dr. Nancy Mergler
ASSISTANT DIRECTOR:	Dr. David Gross
ADDRESS:	Honors Program 347 Cate Center Drive University of Oklahoma Norman, OK 73019-0641
TELEPHONE:	(405) 325-5291
TUITION (FEES)*:	IN-STATE: $1,080 (incl.) OUT-OF-STATE: $3,480 (incl.) * These tuition rates apply for underclass students. Tuition is higher for upperclass students.
TOWN & CAMPUS:	Fair
INTELLECTUAL SETTING:	Poor
ENTRANCE REQUIREMENTS:	Easy
PROGRAM QUALITY:	Fair
OVERALL EVALUATION:	★

▶ The University of Oklahoma (OU) has 20,000 students and is located in Norman. Aside from football, basketball, and the Greek system, there is not much to be said either for the university or its setting. It is fueled by petrodollars, and while a strong oil market means a strong university, the market has unfortunately been weak lately. More significantly, the domination of the state by the oil industry has led to the domination of the campus by departments associated with the industry. The humanities and liberal arts are therefore weak at OU, while geology, land management, and petroleum engineering are strong. So if you love big-time college football and want to major in petroleum engineering, this is the place to go.

Admission to the OU Honors Program is not difficult. Applicants must have an SAT score of 1100 or higher (27 or higher on the ACT) *or* rank in the top 10 percent of their high school graduating class. Successful applicants tend to be above these minimum requirements:

UNIVERSITY OF OKLAHOMA

the 1991 freshman class had an average SAT score of slightly better than 1180 (29 ACT). This is a remarkable achievement given the quality and orientation of the university, and it testifies to the relative strength of the Honors Program.

Applicants must first be admitted to the university, after which they submit the Honors Program application, a simple and easy form. Also required is an essay of 400 to 500 words in which high school seniors are asked to describe their most intellectually challenging experience, write about what it means to be an educated person, or describe the most disconcerting intellectual disagreement they have ever had.

Students may elect to take up to six credits of honors courses per semester, or more, but only with the permission of the program advisors. To complete the program, they must take at least 20 credits of honors courses, or seven classes, and maintain a cumulative GPA of 3.25. (On average, OU honors students take 35 credits of honors courses.) At least 12 honors credits must be taken outside the student's major, a minimum of three credits must be in an interdisciplinary colloquium, and five credits must be in honors reading and research. This last course is really a guided research project designed to produce a paper of publishable quality.

The Honors Program at OU has its own building, Honors House, that contains not only the offices of the program but also houses 180 students, including about half the freshmen admitted to the program annually. Meals and informal get-togethers with faculty members occur here. In 1991 additional housing facilities were provided for upperclass honors students in two buildings adjacent to Honors House.

Approximately 350 new freshmen are admitted into the Honors Program each year, and the total number of students participating in the program is 1,200. Of these, about 10 percent major in the humanities and the rest major in business, engineering, mathematics and the natural sciences, education, and the social sciences. Women make up 49 percent of the total students, African-Americans are 4 percent, Hispanics are 4 percent, Asian-Americans are 4 percent, and Native Americans are another 4 percent. About 20 percent of the students come from out of state, mainly from neighboring Texas, Arkansas, and Kansas but also from Colorado and the Chicago area.

Costs at OU are low: in-state tuition for underclassmen is $45 a credit and $48 for upperclassmen. For out-of-state students it is $145 for underclassmen and $160.75 for upperclassmen. Therefore, an out-of-state freshman taking 24 credits can expect to pay an annual tuition of $3,480. Fees are nominal, and full room and board in an air-conditioned dormitory is about $3,400 annually. Total costs at OU for an out-of-state student are under $7,500, making OU a relatively inexpensive university.

The Honors Program at the University of Oklahoma is not outstanding, but it is solid and it does remarkably well given its surroundings. These, however, are a serious drawback. The university is mediocre and intellectual life in Norman is not on a par with that in Madison, Berkeley, Ann Arbor, or Amherst. There is nowhere to go if things get boring. ■

UNIVERSITY OF OREGON

PROGRAM:	Honors College
DIRECTOR:	Prof. Barbara Pope
ADMISSIONS COORDINATOR:	Ms. Carol Giantonio
ADDRESS:	Clark Honors College 320 Chapman Hall University of Oregon Eugene, OR 97403
TELEPHONE:	(503) 346-5414
TUITION (FEES):	IN-STATE $2,810 (incl.) OUT-OF-STATE $10,030 (incl.)
TOWN & CAMPUS:	Fair
INTELLECTUAL SETTING:	Fair
ENTRANCE REQUIREMENTS:	Competitive
PROGRAM QUALITY:	Good
OVERALL EVALUATION:	★★

▶ With 18,000 students, the University of Oregon (UO) is one of the smaller PAC-10 schools. Recently, UO has attracted Californians who want a less hectic pace or who are skeptical about the stability of the California system of higher education. Beginning in the 1980s the university made a swing back to preprofessional education, so today business administration is one of the most popular majors on campus. Eugene is not a large city, and the environment around the campus is suburban, suggesting that it might be dull, but *Sunset* magazine (in October 1992) argued that Eugene is one of the best college towns in the United States, and we will take their word for it. Oregon is known as a good party school, with a strong Greek system.

The entry-level, university-wide honors program has entrance requirements that are competitive but flexible. Oregon looks for at least a 1200 on the SAT, and the average Honors College student has an SAT score of 1240 and a high school GPA of 3.7, but students who do not meet these standards will be seriously considered if they have other strengths.

Oregon is very much interested in individual students who show promise of distinguishing themselves. A required essay asks for a critical evaluation of an important educational experience. Specific recommendations from high school teachers pointing out innovative students are prized. February 1 is the Honors College application deadline; the deadline is March 1 for the University of Oregon. These are separate application procedures.

About one-third of all courses are taken in the Honors College, which tends to be front-loaded. Oregon operates on a quarter system, with the fourth quarter being summer school. All honors students take three quarters, or 12 credits, of western history and an additional 12 credits of western literature. According to their interests, students in the first two years are then channeled into three-quarter sequences of mathematics, science, social sciences, or arts and letters. It reasonably may be assumed that at least 27 credits of honors courses are taken in the first two years.

Honors classes are small, with a maximum of 25 students, and they are taught in seminar style by full-time faculty. The Honors College has five resident faculty members, two each in western history and western literature. Much of their time is spent advising students, and this advisement structure constitutes the backbone of the program. By choice, there is no dormitory for honors students, but in the Chapman Hall offices of the Honors College there is a lounge, a computer lab, a small library, and a kitchen for the exclusive use of honors students. Upperclass honors students are required to take two 400-level colloquia, and their education culminates in a senior thesis.

The cost of the Oregon honors program is not low: In-state students pay $970 per quarter, or $2,810 annually, and out-of-state students pay $3,010 per quarter, or $10,030 annually. That's the bad news. The good news is that the University of Oregon has what appears to be a very good program; it is well conceived, adequately staffed, and liberally administered. It is well worth considering by any qualified applicant. ∎

PENNSYLVANIA STATE UNIVERSITY

PROGRAM:	University Scholars Program
DIRECTOR:	Prof. Gerard A. Hauser
ASSISTANT DIRECTOR:	Dr. Marilyn Keat
ADDRESS:	University Scholars Program Penn State University 214 Willard Building University Park, PA 16802-2801
TELEPHONE:	(814) 865-2060
TUITION (FEES):	**IN-STATE** $4,752 (incl.) **OUT-OF-STATE** $10,100 (incl.)
TOWN & CAMPUS:	Fair
INTELLECTUAL SETTING:	Good
ENTRANCE REQUIREMENTS:	Very Competitive
PROGRAM QUALITY:	Excellent
OVERALL EVALUATION:	★ ★ ★

▶ The main Penn State campus is located in University Park, about halfway between Philadelphia and Pittsburgh in the middle of rural Pennsylvania. The campus is very nice, and the town basically serves the university. While Penn State is an excellent school, it should be noted that it is predominantly devoted to science and engineering; the liberal arts, while good, are in a distinctly secondary position. Joe Paterno's football team reigns supreme, and the Greek system is very strong.

Entrance requirements to the University Scholars Program are very competitive, but flexible. The mean SAT score for honors students is 1370, with an average unweighted high school GPA of 3.8. Such statistics suggest that Penn State is looking for, and getting, very high quality students. Penn State regards itself as a research university, and the University Scholars Program is strongly adapted to research-oriented students.

We were told that Penn State is definitely flexible in its honors admissions. Although 80 percent of applicants have an SAT score of 1300 or above, Penn State does accept students who have scored in the 1200 to 1300 range, but very few below 1200. Given the uniformly high SAT and high school GPA statistics, the decisive factor in gaining admission is the essay applicants are asked to write. Here again, Penn State is looking for sheer intellectual talent rather than novelty of experience or a distinctive cultural background. We were told that the essay should demonstrate an ability to express ideas and develop arguments.

Only 10 percent of entering students state an intention to major in liberal arts, a percentage that doubles later on as a consequence of students entering laterally. Most entering honors freshmen (65 percent) intend to major in science and engineering.

The University Scholars Program is flexible in its structure. Students are required to take three honors courses annually, which must add up to at least seven credits. In practice, typical freshman honors students take five or six honors courses in each of their first and second years. These courses, comprising 20 to 25 honors students, are taught by full-time instructors in a seminar format that offers an intense educational experience.

Equally significantly, each student has an honors advisor and is required to work out an annual program reflecting his or her goals. Honors students may waive introductory courses in favor of more challenging upper-level courses, or modify their graduation requirements. The Integrated Undergraduate-Graduate option allows them to pursue advanced degrees simultaneously with their undergraduate studies. Because Penn State is a decentralized university, the honors advisors are located in individual colleges or departments rather than in the honors program itself.

In the junior year, honors students begin work on a senior thesis, which is the focal point of the program in the upperclass years. Usually the thesis is done within the student's major with a thesis advisor (the second honors advisor) from the department of that major. The thesis is worth six credits and is counted toward an upperclass requirement of 14 credits for honors students. Retention in the program is based on regular participation and the achievement of a 3.2 GPA each semester.

One distinctive aspect of the Penn State program is its residence facilities. About 450 honors students are housed in two dormitories, Beaver Hall and Atherton Hall. The latter has apartments for distinguished visitors and a resident faculty house mentor. It is also equipped with a computer room, darkroom, kitchen, and library.

Using these resources, the University Scholars Program organizes dinner seminars, receptions, and discussions with faculty members and visiting scholars, and it is here that Penn State fosters community in its honors program. Students are encouraged to participate in community service projects initiated through the SAIL (Service, Achievement, Initiative, Leadership) policy. They regularly participate in honors study abroad, and a two-week London Study Tour is offered.

The Penn State University Scholars Program has between 1,200 and 1,300 students. Of these, about 50 percent are women, but, interestingly, many of the women are lateral entrants to the program, coming in only after having established a good record in liberal arts. At the freshman entry level, women make up a smaller percentage.

Penn State reports that its admissions procedure does not take ethnicity or gender into account, so it has no statistics. When pressed for some sense of the ethnic and racial mix of students, officials at Penn State said that typically 10 percent of incoming students are minority, with African-Americans making up 2 percent of the students in the program. In order to secure minority participation, Penn State each year awards 20 "early-offer" Academic Excellence Scholarships to minority students still in high school. Out-of-state students make up 30 percent of the participants in the program, and as expected many of these come from states near Pennsylvania. Students from New York and New Jersey are especially well represented in the program.

Penn State tends to be expensive for a state university. The in-state tuition is $4,752 annually, and out-of-state students pay $10,100 annually. However, nearly all successful honors applicants qualify for Academic Excellence Scholarships of $2,376 annually, which are automatically renewed if students remain in good standing in the program.

On balance, the Penn State honors program is excellent for a very scholarly high school senior who wants to be challenged, exposed to high-quality professors, and oriented toward a research/creative experience embodied in a thesis. For this kind of person, Penn State's is one of the best honors programs at a state university in the United States. The only real disadvantage of the Penn State program is the location of University Park, but if one likes hilly countryside, this may not present a problem. ■

RUTGERS UNIVERSITY

PROGRAM:	General Honors Program
DIRECTOR:	Prof. Terry Matilsky
ASSOCIATE DIRECTOR:	Ms. Muffin Lord
ADDRESS:	Director General Honors Program Rutgers College Milledoler Hall College Avenue Campus New Brunswick, NJ 08903
TELEPHONE:	(908) 932-7964
TUITION (FEES):	**IN-STATE** $3,433 ($854) **OUT-OF-STATE** $6,623 ($854)
TOWN & CAMPUS:	Good
INTELLECTUAL SETTING:	Good
ENTRANCE REQUIREMENTS:	Very Competitive
PROGRAM QUALITY:	Fair
OVERALL EVALUATION:	★

▶ Rutgers is the State University of New Jersey, and Rutgers College is one of its internal units. Like William & Mary College in Virginia, Rutgers College is an old private college that was acquired by the state to function as the core of the state university. Rutgers played the first intercollegiate football game (against neighboring Princeton) in the 1870s, and the campus still retains much of its original charm. The city of New Brunswick has seen better days, but its great advantage is that it is one hour from both New York City and Philadelphia.

The program described here is that of Rutgers College, the largest by far of the four liberal arts colleges for undergraduates. Douglass (a women's college) and Livingston Colleges also have honors programs, but each of these is less than half the size of Rutgers College. Information about the Douglass College honors program may be obtained from Prof. Alice Crozier at (908) 932-9626 and about the Livingston College program from Prof. Marty Glisserman at (908) 932-8094.

RUTGERS UNIVERSITY

Entrance requirements to the General Honors Program of Rutgers College are very competitive. A minimum SAT score of 1300, with at least 620 on the verbal, is expected, as well as standing in the top 10 percent of one's high school graduating class. In addition, an essay is required in which it is expected that the applicant will demonstrate superior writing and thinking skills. Rutgers evidently wants creative and dynamic students, and it can probably get them by virtue of its location.

There are slightly more than 400 students in the Rutgers College honors program, and men and women are about equally represented. Minority representation in the program is between 7 and 8 percent, or about 30 students.

The chief characteristic of the program is that it is not especially demanding. Only three seminars are required over a four-year period, one each in the humanities, the social sciences, and math/science. Students usually fulfill these requirements in the first two years. Twelve seminars per semester are offered to choose from, taught by any full-time faculty member who submits a successful proposal. These seminars cannot be substituted for General Education (core) requirements.

In addition, students are expected to do junior-year and senior-year projects. The former may involve spending two semesters doing independent research, community service, a junior year or semester abroad, or a semester or year at another university. The senior year project is more intellectual and involves doing a senior thesis, pursuing departmental honors, taking graduate-level courses, or doing the General Honors Interdisciplinary Thesis. Normally, the senior thesis is the equivalent of six credits' work.

Students must maintain a 3.0 GPA to remain in the program, but graduation from the program requires a 3.4 GPA. There is no honors dormitory, but housing for honors students is reserved in two dormitories.

Rutgers College, like Rutgers University, is inexpensive. Annual tuition for in-state students is $3,433 and $6,623 for out-of-state students. There are many small scholarships available to make it even less expensive. Although these are university-wide scholarships, honors students should be especially good competitors for these awards.

The weakness of the Rutgers honors program is that it does not replace the underclass core requirements with small classes taught by full-time faculty. Most of the honors experience is in the three required seminars, and this is not very much. The options available for the junior-year project are not distinctly honors-related, and may be taken by any qualified student, as may the senior-year options. The Rutgers College program basically boils down to only three exclusively honors seminars. ■

UNIVERSITY OF RHODE ISLAND	

PROGRAM:	The Honors Program
DIRECTOR:	Dr. Maury Klein
HONORS ADVISOR:	Prof. Winifred Caldwell
ADDRESS:	The Honors Program Taft Hall University of Rhode Island Kingston, RI 02881
TELEPHONE:	(401) 792-2303
TUITION (FEES):	IN-STATE: $3,822 (incl.) OTHER NEW ENGLAND STATES: $5,009 (incl.) OUTSIDE NEW ENGLAND: $10,606 (incl.)
TOWN & CAMPUS:	Good
INTELLECTUAL SETTING:	Fair
ENTRANCE REQUIREMENTS:	Easy
PROGRAM QUALITY:	Fair
OVERALL EVALUATION:	★

▶ Kingston is a very small town that is strongly dominated by the University of Rhode Island, which is itself small, with a total enrollment of only 12,000 students. Because Rhode Island is a small state, a large portion of students either commute or go home on weekends, which puts something of a damper on social life. The quality of intellectual life on campus is fair. One distinct advantage of URI in Kingston is its escape hatches: the ocean is only a few miles away; Providence, with Brown University, is 40 miles away; and Boston, with all its cultural advantages, is only 90 miles out of town.

Discussion of entrance requirements for the Honors Program is difficult because in a technical sense Rhode Island has none. The only stated requirement is that high school seniors be in the top 10 percent of their high school graduating class or, failing this, have a recommendation from their high school principal or guidance counselor stating that they are capable of doing honors work. The Honors Program recruits its students from the general pool of applicants accepted at the university; students are not actively recruited until they are already enrolled at URI.

The SAT score currently plays no role in the current selection process, but the present Director, Dr. Maury Klein, hopes to see the SAT score become one of several variables determining who is admitted to the program. Of course, this means that students would be recruited at an earlier stage. Dr. Klein gives every indication that he would prefer the Rhode Island program to move in the direction of more conventional honors programs in other respects as well.

The Honors Program's stated requirements are minimal and are relatively unstructured. To earn the transcript designation "Completed the University Honors Program," participating students must have attained an overall GPA of 3.2 at the university and have taken at least 15 credits of honors courses. These should include at least one three-credit 100-level course, one three-credit Honors Colloquium, one 300-level tutorial, and six credits at the 400 level. The 400-level requirement may be satisfied either with a six-credit senior honors project or a three-credit honors project coupled with a three-credit senior thesis. Students normally take a wide variety of credits over their career in the Honors Program.

Needless to say, class sizes in the Rhode Island honors program are small, but this takes on a new meaning at the University of Rhode Island. Most 100-level honors courses have fewer than 15 students, and upper-division courses are even smaller. Most 300-level honors courses are limited to eight students, and the three- or six-credit senior thesis requirement is actually a one-on-one experience between student and professor. All of the faculty who teach in the program are said to be of top quality; they apply to teach in the program and are selected or rejected by a committee of which the Honors Program Director is chair.

The University of Rhode Island has a total of 180 students participating in the Honors Program. Of these about two-thirds are women and about 5 percent are minorities. More specifically, there are three or four African-Americans and the balance are Asian-Americans. About 50 percent of the students in the program are from out of state, and while many of these are from neighboring Massachusetts and Connecticut, a surprising number are from New York and New Jersey. The University of Rhode Island depends heavily on tuition for income and therefore prizes out-of-state students, who pay higher tuition rates.

There is no specific housing for honors students, but they may request to be placed in quiet dormitories or to live with other honors students.

It should be noted that tuition at the University of Rhode Island is high, but with an unusual twist. For out-of-state students, tuition and fees are $10,606 annually, but there is a regional tuition-and-fees figure of $5,009 for students from other New England states. The status of this lower tuition rate is dubious, however, so interested students should inquire further. In-state tuition and fees are $3,882. There is scholarship money available for honors students.

The Honors Program at the University of Rhode Island is in a state of flux. The current program is competitive but not especially difficult to get into, and it is skeletal in its requirements. It is moving toward more conventional standards, and so it might be worth looking at for a student attracted to URI for other reasons. The campus and town are not great, but if things get bad, Boston is not far away. ■

UNIVERSITY OF SOUTH CAROLINA	
PROGRAM:	The Honors College
DIRECTOR:	Dean William Mould
ASSOCIATE DIRECTOR:	Associate Dean James Stiver
ADDRESS:	The Honors College Harper 201 University of South Carolina Columbia, SC 29208
TELEPHONE:	(803) 777-8102
TUITION (FEES):	**IN-STATE** $1,545 (incl.) **OUT-OF-STATE** $3,904 (incl.)
TOWN & CAMPUS:	Good
INTELLECTUAL LIFE:	Good
ENTRANCE REQUIREMENTS:	Competitive
PROGRAM QUALITY:	Excellent
OVERALL EVALUATION:	★★

▶ The campus of the University of South Carolina (USC) is charming, especially around the "Horseshoe," which is the campus center. Intellectual life is good, and the Koge Center for the Arts offers a distinctive music program. In theory, the campus is dry, but with a strong Greek system, one can be sure that lots of drinking gets done. There are African-Americans as well as whites on this campus, which dates from before the old Confederacy, but, unfortunately, separation of races is practiced and tacitly accepted on both sides. USC is a real southern university, more so than other more cosmopolitan universities like those in North Carolina or Virginia. It keeps a distinctly regional feel but still manages to have many of the advantages of its more illustrious counterparts.

The first thing to note is that USC has an Honors College rather than an honors program, such terminology generally indicating relatively high status and funding. As one of 17 colleges on the USC campus, the Honors College is headed by a dean rather than by a director (who reports to a dean), which means that he or she can do battle at a higher level, usually with more favorable results. The Dean at USC, Dr. William Mould, has been running the program since the 1970s, and hence the Honors College has an impressive leadership continuity.

Admission to the Honors College is relatively simple. Students must first apply for general admission to the University. The applications of those who succeed are then reviewed, and if it is thought that they qualify for the Honors College, they are sent a separate admissions package. The two basic requirements for admission are a score of at least 1200 on the SAT (an ACT score of 28) and class standing in the top 10 percent of one's high school graduating class. Students not qualifying on one of the criteria may ask for an alternative mode of selection.

Also required is an interview with an honors faculty member (usually one of the core of advisors for the College), a writing sample, and a writing assessment from a high school English instructor. No written essay is required.

The curriculum of the Honors College is both structured and unstructured. On the structured side, students are required to take 44 credits of honors courses of the 120 credits needed to graduate from USC. One of these courses must be in analytical reasoning, two courses each in one science, English, history of civilization, and humanities/social sciences, as well as one course devoted to a senior thesis. Freshmen normally take two or three honors courses.

Alternatively, USC offers a more intensive honors program, called B.AR.SC., or the *Baccalaureus Artium et Scientiae*, which is open to existing honors students who have compiled a GPA of at least 3.6 in their freshman year. They are required to complete 68 credits of honors work, which include the same 44 credits required in the regular honors program, a nine-credit senior thesis (six additional credits), and five additional honors courses. This course plan is put together by a committee made up of the Dean, the Associate Dean, two faculty advisors, and the student. The main difference between this program and the conventional honors program is that the B.AR.SC. student does not have a major, which is one of the reasons for the extra depth in the senior thesis.

One important aspect of both honors programs is an internship that provides students with quality experience in fields of their choosing. Especially valuable is the Washington, D.C., Congressional Fellowship, which places eight students each semester in the offices of South Carolina's two senators and six representatives. Participants are said to be doing real work and gaining real experience on Capitol Hill.

The unstructured side of the USC Honors College is actually just a different kind of structure. Although the honors curriculum does not have explicit requirements, there is an intensive advisement program that tailors an educational program to the needs and talents of the individual student. Ideally, this is a better way to do things, but there is some question whether things actually work out as planned.

To retain standing in the Honors College, freshmen must attain an index of at least 3.0, which must be improved incrementally to at least a 3.3 to graduate with honors. Nearly 100 different honors courses are offered each semester, each taught by a full-time instructor. In 1993, the average class size was 17.

There are a total of 750 students participating in the USC Honors College, and 175 new freshmen enter each year. Women make up 50 percent of the total, and 11 percent are from states other than South Carolina. Interestingly, most of the out-of-staters do not come from contiguous states. Part of the reason for this is the attractiveness of some especially strong programs at USC, such as Marine Science.

Minorities make up an indeterminate percentage of the total students in the USC Honors College, including about 5 to 6 percent African-Americans, indicating that USC takes seriously its need to diversify. There are also a small number of Indian and Pakistani students.

Some scholarships are available, and here there is nothing extraordinary to say except the following: by law or tradition, USC charges in-state tuition rates to any student winning a university scholarship of $500 or more. This policy multiplies the worth of the $500 scholarship many times over, so out-of-state students should make sure they make the effort to win a small scholarship.

Housing is available to honors students. Entering freshmen may choose to live in "honors clusters" in regular dormitories, thereby attaining the best (or worst) of both worlds. Upperclass honors students may choose to live in restored residence halls on the Horseshoe, which is the site of the original campus and is much desired by USC students; living on the Horseshoe at USC is like living in Harvard Yard at Harvard University. In 1991–92, 132 Honors College students lived on the Horseshoe, about 18 percent of all honors students. One may also choose to live off campus.

The Honors College at USC is an excellent program. The only disadvantage we see is the University itself, but this is only relatively speaking. USC is not Michigan or Texas, or for that matter UVA or North Carolina. But it is still a better place to be than many U.S. state universities. The honors program itself is close to ideal: It is both structured and unstructured, and where it is unstructured, it is characterized by advisement that results in tailored structuring. Students are given an orderly, high-quality education from beginning to end. ■

NEW COLLEGE OF THE UNIVERSITY OF SOUTH FLORIDA

PROGRAM:	New College
DIRECTOR:	Mr. David L. Anderson
ASSOCIATE DIRECTOR:	Miss Kathleen Killian
ADDRESS:	New College University of South Florida 5700 North Tamiami Trail Sarasota, FL 34243-2197
TELEPHONE:	(813) 359-4269
TUITION (FEES):	**IN-STATE** $2,030 (incl.) **OUT-OF-STATE** $7,913 (incl.)
TOWN & CAMPUS:	Fair
INTELLECTUAL SETTING:	Fair
ENTRANCE REQUIREMENTS:	Competitive
PROGRAM QUALITY:	Good
OVERALL EVALUATION:	★★

▶ Sarasota is a wonderful place, but it is not a college town; however beautiful its beaches, mansions, and palm trees, it does not seem the right setting for learning. This is due less to the distracting climate than to the absence of a critical mass of intellectual talent such as one finds in Austin or Madison. New College is far away from USF in Tampa, so it does not have the benefits of a large state university campus.

New College was a small private college that merged with USF in 1975. It is now part of the state university system, but it also retains its separate identity. Entrance requirements to New College are competitive but flexible. Applicants are expected to have completed an academic high school program including four years of English, three years of science, three years of math, three years of social science, two consecutive years of the same foreign language, and four other academic electives. A high SAT score is also expected. While it appears that 1200 is the lower threshold, more than 20 percent of last year's successful applicants scored below this. More than half last year's successful applicants were in the top 10 percent of their high school graduating class, leaving a good portion that were not.

The program at New College is simple and innovative. Students are treated as individuals capable of making their own decisions, and are expected to negotiate written contracts with faculty advisors. The requirement for graduation is seven successful contracts (that is, seven successful semesters). There are no grades, but students are evaluated on their performance by a faculty committee at the end of each semester.

It must be remembered that New College is an honors college, not an honors program, and it is unique among honors colleges by not being located on the parent campus. The best way to look at New College is to treat it as a private liberal arts college such as Haverford or Reed. The appropriate question is therefore not whether the program is front- or back-loaded, but whether the programs offered are of high quality. New College is organized into three tracks—humanities, natural sciences, and social sciences—and all appear to be solid.

New College has slightly under 500 students. Of these, just over one-half are women and 11 percent are minorities, including 2 percent African-Americans. New College is very forthcoming about minorities, claiming that it was the first racially integrated college in Florida and inviting minorities to apply. About 45 percent of New College students come from out of state, many from nonsouthern states.

There would seem to be no reason to mention honors housing at New College, since all the students are honors students, but it should be noted that the main complex of dormitories was designed by the renowned architect I.M. Pei, and provides an assortment of double rooms that maximize privacy.

Even better news is the cost of New College. In-state students pay $2,030 annually and out-of-state students pay $7,913. When one considers that New College is for all practical purposes a small liberal arts college, this is a bargain.

Our stated preference is for honors programs rather than honors colleges, and consequently, we prefer honors colleges to be on-campus rather than off. But if one wants a small high-quality liberal arts college in a pleasant atmosphere, this is the place. For our purposes, New College can be compared to Miami University of Ohio, the University of New Hampshire, or William & Mary of Virginia: All four institutions are small, high-quality schools comparable to the best small private liberal arts colleges. ■

UNIVERSITY OF TENNESSEE

PROGRAM:	The Honors Programs
DIRECTOR:	Dr. William B. Wheeler
ASSOCIATE DIRECTOR:	Dr. Dorothy Hendricks
ADDRESS:	University Honors Program F101 Melrose Hall The University of Tennessee Knoxville, TN 37916
TELEPHONE:	(615) 974-7875
TUITION (FEES):	IN-STATE: No tuition ($1,982) OUT-OF-STATE: $3,780 ($1,982)
TOWN & CAMPUS:	Fair
INTELLECTUAL SETTING:	Fair
ENTRANCE REQUIREMENTS:	Very Competitive
PROGRAM QUALITY:	Fair to Good
OVERALL EVALUATION:	★★

▶ Knoxville lacks the attractions of a college town but does have the distractions one might expect of a larger-than-average city. The surrounding countryside is beautiful, as are the more distant Great Smoky Mountains. The University of Tennessee is oriented toward engineering and characterized by a lot of partying, and unfortunately the liberal arts are not all that one might wish. Given that entrance requirements are low and the student body is mainly in-state, the University does not offer a stimulating intellectual environment.

Tennessee is one of the few state universities where it makes sense to discuss the honors program *before* one considers the entrance requirements. The reason for this is that *all* of the students in the program are on scholarship, and the scholarship programs differ—hence the designation "The Honors Programs." This is really a composite of several scholarship programs.

By far the most attractive is the Whittle Scholars Program, which offers full scholarships ($7,000 per year), renewable for five years (including one extra year of international work/travel/study), to 20 students a year, about four of whom are from out of state. Out-of-state tuition is waived for non-Tennesseans. The selection standards for this scholarship are high: a high school GPA of 3.25 or above and an ACT of 31 or an SAT of 1300. High school seniors must be nominated by January 1 and complete their application by February 1. Forty-five semifinalists will be chosen and interviewed in early March, and final selections will be made on March 15. Interested high school students should write or phone the honors program.

The program for the Whittle Scholars includes seminars, small classes, special advisors, off-campus career mentors, monthly dinners with outstanding speakers, and a full academic year abroad. The Whittle Scholars Program emphasizes leadership, and, in this respect, it might be compared to the University of Montana's honors program. Whittle Scholars are required to take the Whittle Seminar in the first year, which deals with current events in the fall and leadership in the spring. Participating students must maintain an overall 3.25 GPA to remain in the program.

The most attractive feature of the Whittle Scholars Program is the year abroad. Students are individually placed in work/travel/study programs that fit their academic and career goals. Whittle Scholars have worked in Tokyo, studied at the London School of Economics, worked in missions in Kenya and Australia, and organized youth programs in Russia.

A sister program, the Tennessee Scholars Program, awards scholarships of $4,000, renewable for four or five years, to 25 high school seniors or transfer students, few of whom are out-of-staters (out-of-state tuition is *not* waived for Tennessee Scholars). This program is not a consolation prize given to disappointed semifinalists in the Whittle competition; it is based primarily on test scores, and they tend to be higher: 32 on the ACT and 1350 on the SAT. Application to the Whittle Program doubles as application to the Tennessee Scholars Program. Here, too, the retention standard is an overall 3.25 GPA.

The program includes a Tennessee Scholars seminar each semester (one credit), a minimum of one additional honors seminar each semester in the first four semesters, and an independent senior project. Interested high school seniors who are not applying to the Whittle Program but are interested in the Tennessee Scholars Program should write to the address in the information box at the beginning of this entry.

Recipients of the Roddy, Bonham, Neyland, Holt, and Reeder-Siler scholarships, which total about 16 in number, are called Chancellor's Scholars. The entrance requirements and retention standards for this group vary according to the individual scholarship. Chancellor's Scholars are required to complete four honors seminars in the first two years of residence, an additional one-credit Tennessee Seminar each semester in residence, and a senior honors research project.

Some highly qualified students manage to get into the University of Tennessee without being given prestigious scholarship aid. They are called College Scholars, and are not technically in the honors program. Even here the opportunity to receive a scholarship still exists, but it is deferred to the end of sophomore year, when Nielsen Scholarships are available to students who have achieved good academic records. The requirements of the College Scholars Program may be taken as the basic honors program: the weekly one-hour scholars seminar is required as well as the senior project. Whittle Scholars and Tennessee Scholars may also become College Scholars, although Whittle Scholars are not eligible for the Nielsen Scholarships.

The Tennessee programs are obviously complex. The minimal program of the College Scholars is evidently extremely thin, consisting basically of nothing more than the one-hour seminar plus a lot of consultation. This program has not been considered in our overall evaluation since it is beyond the aegis of the Tennessee honors programs. At the opposite extreme, the Whittle Scholars Program is rich and demanding. Tennessee is really a case study of the rich getting richer and the poor getting poorer, so applicants must think carefully about the level at which they want to enter.

Tennessee accepts 45 to 60 new freshmen each year, and the total number of students in the programs is 180. Of these, 50 percent are women and 8 percent are minorities, of whom nine are African-Americans and six are Asian-Americans. Only a small percentage are from out of state, and since the University of Tennessee is one of the largest state universities in the south and Tennessee borders on several other southern states, most of the out-of-staters are from neighboring states.

The University of Tennessee is inexpensive as state universities go. The annual out-of-state tuition is $3,780, but fees are $1,982, no small figure. In-staters pay no tuition but pay the same fees as out-of-staters. This makes the University of Tennessee attractive, especially to in-staters, and enhances the value of the scholarships given out.

It is difficult to tell whether in-staters or out-of-staters have the advantage as applicants, since the proportion of scholarships given to out-of-staters corresponds to the lower number of out-of-state applicants. Eighty percent of Whittle Scholarships must be given to Tennessee residents. When we asked whether Tennessee welcomes applicants from outside the South, we received a less-than-enthusiastic reply: yes, but only if they meet admissions standards. It is well to keep in mind that the Tennessee programs are new and growing, and so policy is in flux.

There is no special housing for honors students at the University of Tennessee, but as compensation the program's administrators are trying to develop better facilities at their offices (a well-equipped honors lounge).

Obviously, the Honors Programs at the University of Tennessee are a mixed package calling for a good deal of judgment on the part of the applicant. The first question is whether a qualified applicant wants to spend several years in Knoxville. The answer to this question, it seems to us, may be determined by financial considerations. The Whittle and Tennessee Scholars programs are very good, and this, too, may help determine the answer. ■

UNIVERSITY OF TEXAS AT AUSTIN

PROGRAM:	Plan II Honors Program
DIRECTOR:	Prof. Paul Woodruff
ASSISTANT TO DIRECTOR:	Ms. Karen Bordelon
ADDRESS:	Plan II Honors Program WMB 116 UT Austin Austin, TX 78712
TELEPHONE:	(512) 471-1442
TUITION (FEES):	**IN-STATE** $1,460 (incl.) **OUT-OF-STATE** $4,996 (incl.)
TOWN & CAMPUS:	Excellent
INTELLECTUAL SETTING:	Excellent
ENTRANCE REQUIREMENTS:	Very Competitive
PROGRAM QUALITY:	Excellent
OVERALL EVALUATION:	★ ★ ★

▶ The University of Texas (UT) at Austin is large even by the standards of state universities. It has 49,000 students and is located in the state capital, which also happens to be a good college town, comparable to Madison, Ann Arbor, or Amherst. The university is well endowed, has one of the largest university libraries in America (six million volumes) and ranks high among universities in the number of Nobel Prize winners on its faculty. In brief, this is one of the better state universities. As such it provides an excellent setting for its honors program.

The University of Texas actually has many honors programs, but most of them are small or cater to lateral entry by students already enrolled. Plan II is an entry-level program for liberal arts students that dates back to the founding in 1935 of a small, low-key "Great Books" program (Plan I). This provided the basis for what later became an honors program, now upgraded to Plan II.

The entrance requirements for Plan II are high but flexible. There is no stated minimum SAT, but 72 percent of this year's admitted students scored above 1300, and the average SAT score for

UNIVERSITY OF TEXAS AT AUSTIN

1992 was 1328, down slightly from the year before. More than 75 percent of newly admitted students were in the top 5 percent of their high school graduating classes, and an astounding 50 percent were National Merit Finalists. Essays are required, but not an interview, although the Director wants to begin having them. Standards are flexible, meaning that both overachievers and underachievers are considered.

The program administrators insist that they are also looking for an enriched student profile, describing applicants who are intellectually well rounded, spirited talkers, and good writers. They see themselves as competing for a national elite who are also applying to Rice, Harvard, Vanderbilt, Yale, and Duke.

The Plan II program is front-loaded, meaning that most of the honors experience is in the freshman and sophomore years. Students take most of their core courses in small sections with other honors students taught by the best faculty (teaching assistants are used solely as discussion leaders at UT). This year, for example, 11 sections of freshman honors English composition are being given, with between 15 and 20 students per section. Students take the majority of their honors courses in these first two years, thereby establishing peer relations that will see them through the duration of their undergraduate careers. During the last two years, most students complete the Plan II program as a major in liberal arts. Some students choose conventional majors in addition, in effect creating a double major. Required in these last two years are two junior seminars, one senior thesis forum, and a senior thesis.

The Plan II Honors Program is enriched with an impressive extracurricular program of activities. UT is a very strong research university, and retreats and special seminars featuring noted researchers are designed for Plan II students. In addition, informal gatherings called "Voltaire's Coffee" are organized two or three times a month in the homes of faculty members. There are also Honors Center Evening Seminars, which usually bring in outside speakers for all honors programs and the Plan II Students Association sponsors picnics and parties.

There are 750 students in the program. About 150 new freshmen and 25 transfer students are admitted each year. The balance between men and women is just about even, tilting slightly toward the male side. Approximately 8 percent of Plan II students major in engineering, and 15 percent are premed. About 80 percent are from Texas and

IVY LEAGUE PROGRAMS AT STATE SCHOOL PRICES

the other 20 percent from out of state, many coming from the east coast. There are not many foreign students in the program. A surprisingly high percentage of students are minorities: about 7 percent are African-American, 8 percent Hispanic, and 10 percent Asian-Americans. The attrition rate is low, with only about 10 students leaving the program yearly.

Tuition at the university is low to start with. In 1993 it was $1,460 for in-state students and $4,996 for out-of-state students annually. Room, board, and books add up to another $4,500, making Texas one of the better bargains in U.S. higher education. Scholarship aid for Plan II students is impressive. National Merit Semifinalists from out-of-state are granted in-state tuition rates as well as scholarships of $750 each. All National Merit Finalists are in addition given $700 to $2,000 in financial aid. Finally, there are other grants available, such as small scholarships from "Texas Exes" clubs, which are alumni associations throughout the United States.

Honors housing is available but limited. Two small, attractive dormitories, Andrews and Carothers, have recently been renovated and designated as honors dormitories. Plan II may designate about 25 to 30 students for these dormitories. Other Plan II freshmen are set up in other campus dormitories (one of which is large enough to have its own zip code) or in private dormitories near the campus. Housing in Austin is charming and very inexpensive.

Having a long tradition, Plan II has a great deal of prestige on campus and in the state of Texas. Law school attracts about 20 percent of its Plan II graduates, 15 percent go on to medical school, about 20 percent end up in the business world, and 45 percent pursue graduate degrees. Because of its affiliations in Texas, which is, as ever, something of a world apart, career prospects for Plan II graduates are among the best in the nation.

The Plan II Honors Program is in all respects excellent. Moreover, it is a nearly perfect example of a front-loaded honors program, one that directs most of its resources to laying a foundation in the first two years and then leaves students to engage in maximum self-realization. It is one of the least expensive state programs, not just relatively but absolutely. The University of Michigan, for example, also has an excellent program, but its cost is among the highest at public universities, and so, all things considered, Texas comes out looking better. This is one of the best bargains in American higher education. ■

TEXAS A&M UNIVERSITY	

PROGRAM:	University Honors Program
DIRECTOR:	Dr. Dale T. Knobel
ASSOCIATE DIRECTOR:	Dr. Susanna Finnel
PROGRAM COORDINATOR:	Ms. Julie Cowley
ADDRESS:	University Honors Program Texas A&M University College Station, TX 77843-4233
TELEPHONE:	(409) 845-1957
TUITION (FEES):	**IN-STATE** $780 ($768) **OUT-OF-STATE** $4,860 ($768)
TOWN & CAMPUS:	Good
INTELLECTUAL SETTING:	Fair
ENTRANCE REQUIREMENTS:	Competitive
PROGRAM QUALITY:	Good
OVERALL EVALUATION:	★★

▶ By any standard an excellent university, Texas A&M is located in central Texas in a city of 38,000. The university itself has 34,000 students, and its long-standing tradition of educating for agricultural, mechanical, and military careers is continued today in a predominantly engineering student body. Recently, however, the liberal arts have been growing rapidly at Texas A&M, and given a flat national market in this area, the university has been able to recruit excellent faculty. Texas A&M is also one of the best universities in the country for studying communications and atomic science.

There is no separate application process for entrance into the University Honors Program. Eligible freshmen rank in the top 10 percent of their high school graduating classes and have attained SAT scores of at least 1150 or ACT scores of 28. Students already enrolled at Texas A&M may enter the program laterally with a cumulative GPR (Grade Point Ratio) of 3.25. All participants must maintain a 3.25 cumulative GPA each semester.

The University Honors Program has a populist cast: Honors students are free to choose to take any honors courses they please. These courses are small sections taught by senior faculty and are designed to emphasize participatory learning. Approximately 150 honors courses are offered each semester. Students who accumulate 22 credits by taking honors courses in the seven areas of the Texas A&M core curriculum are awarded the designation of "Foundation Honors" on their transcripts. (The core requirement at Texas A&M is 48 credits, a comparatively high number.) The 22 honors credits must include three credits each in speech/writing skills, mathematics/logical reasoning, cultural heritage, social science, American government, and American history. There is also a four-credit requirement in the natural sciences. Foundation Honors recognizes the breadth of honors accomplishment.

Students who accumulate 33 to 36 honors credits are awarded the distinction of "University Honors." Here the distribution of credits is different from that in Foundation Honors. For University Honors, students must earn at least six honors credits in the humanities and social sciences, six more credits in basic science or mathematics, and at least 12 credits at the advanced course level. Here, as in Foundation Honors, there is a double retention standard: students must maintain an overall Grade Point Ratio of 3.25 and an honors Grade Point Ratio of 3.0, with no honors course grade of less than a C. University Honors recognizes the depth of their achievement.

Each year the University Honors Program admits about 600 new freshmen. The total number of participating students is 2,600, about 50 percent of whom are women. Minorities make up 15 percent of this year's freshman class, and of these about one-third are African-Americans and two-thirds are Hispanics. Another 5 percent are Asian-Americans, but Texas A&M does not count these students as underrepresented minorities. The percentage of out-of-state students is 18.

Out-of-state tuition and fees are $4,860 annually, while in-state tuition is a mere $780 annually. As at the University of Texas, oil is a major source of revenue for Texas A&M, but recently prices have been down and the state legislature has been raising tuition accordingly. Nonetheless, there is still a good deal of scholarship money available, which is administered by the Office of Honors Programs and Academic Scholarships. So generous are Texas A&M's scholarship programs that they are worth looking at in detail.

There are four major scholarship programs available for incoming freshmen: the President's Endowed Scholarship, the President's Achievement Scholarship, the Lechner Scholarship, and the McFadden Scholarship. Together they provide about 700 scholarships, more than half of which go to incoming honors freshmen. To compete for these awards, students must have minimum SATs of 1250, or 30 on the ACT, and rank in the top 10 percent of their high school classes. The Academic Scholarship Selection Committee ultimately chooses recipients on the basis not only of test scores and class rank but also on the strength of courses taken, recommendations, and school and community leadership. Attainment of a scholarship by out-of-state students also brings with it an out-of-state tuition waiver, which alone is worth more than any of the scholarships! The scholarships range from $2,000 to $5,500 yearly and are renewable for four years. The President's Achievement Scholarship is awarded to African-American and Hispanic students.

Housing at Texas A&M was, but no longer is, a problem, even though on-campus dormitory rooms are available for only about one-third of the students. Off-campus students reside in private residences, fraternities, sororities, and apartment complexes. There is an honors dormitory, with places available to all honors-eligible students who receive major academic scholarships. All four-year academic scholarship holders are guaranteed on-campus housing.

The University Honors Program at Texas A&M is probably as good as it can be, given the circumstances. The main drawback is the predominantly engineering and preprofessional atmosphere in undergraduate studies, something that compels the Honors Program to opt for maximum flexibility. But if you want to study communications or work with people in nuclear science, Texas A&M is a first-rate place to be, and the University Honors Program is a good one. ■

UNIVERSITY OF UTAH

PROGRAM:	Honors Program
DIRECTOR:	Dr. Richard J. Cummings
ASSISTANT DIRECTOR:	Dr. Esther Radinger
ADDRESS:	Honors Program Building 124 University of Utah Salt Lake City, UT 84112
TELEPHONE:	(801) 581-7383
TUITION (FEES):	IN-STATE $2,298 ($100) OUT-OF-STATE $6,795 ($100)
TOWN & CAMPUS:	Good
INTELLECTUAL LIFE:	Good
ENTRANCE REQUIREMENTS:	Easy
PROGRAM QUALITY:	Good
OVERALL EVALUATION:	★★

▶ The University of Utah (U of U) exists in the shadow of the better-known Brigham Young University. Both are large, with more than 20,000 students, and both are attended primarily by Mormons. But here the similarity ends, for where BYU is strict and intensively Mormon, U of U is not. It is a conservative, predominantly Mormon university, but it is much less religious than BYU, and is consciously secularizing its faculty and student body. The University of Utah is also more research-oriented than BYU, so it provides a good setting for an honors program.

Applicants for the Honors Program are expected to have a high school GPA of at least 3.5, and a score of at least 27 or 28 on the ACT, about 1140 on the SAT. The University uses the GPA and the test score to generate a single index, so students with lower GPAs may compensate by doing better on the ACT or SAT, or vice versa.

In order to graduate with an honors degree, students must take at least eight honors courses, although in practice it is virtually impossible to graduate with fewer than 10 honors courses. Incoming students must choose from two sequences of western civilization courses, the less intensive three-quarter sequence lasting a full year and the more intensive five-quarter sequence lasting nearly two years. Students must then take one to three 200-level honors courses, the number depending on how many 100-level courses they have previously taken. For example, a student who has taken three 100-level courses must take three 200-level courses, while a student taking five 100-level courses is only obliged to take one 200-level course. The 200-level courses are more specialized than the 100-level courses.

This complicated formula reflects a simple intention: The Honors Program insists upon an exceptionally solid grounding in the intellectual traditions of the West. By calculation, the honors student is taking six quarters, or two full years, of western civilization courses. Students must also take one or two 300- or 400-level honors courses.

Honors students must also complete a calculus requirement made up of two courses, one quarter of calculus and a second quarter of a course that uses calculus. They are also asked to demonstrate foreign language proficiency, but this is not very difficult to do. For the BA, students must show "fifth quarter" proficiency, and for the BS, "third quarter" proficiency, which roughly works out to less than two years of college-level foreign language study.

Students who complete this sequence of requirements are expected to do so while maintaining a cumulative GPA of at least 3.4 and an honors GPA of at least 3.0. They must also give a "Senior Exit Interview" at least five quarters before they graduate. This is a one-hour interview that provides an opportunity both to assess the program and to fine-tune the participant's senior experience.

There are approximately 1,100 to 1,200 students in the honors program at Utah, and roughly 400 new freshmen are admitted each year. Men and women are about equally represented, and minorities, mainly Hispanics, make up about 12 to 15 percent of the total, another 10 percent if Asian-Americans are included. There are very few African-Americans living in Utah or the contiguous states, so there are very few in this program. But the university is said to be committed to diversity and encourages African-American students to apply.

Out-of-state students make up about 20 percent of the total number of honors students, and the state most strongly represented is neighboring Wyoming. Other contiguous states do not have a significant edge over more distant states. The University of Utah is committed to bringing in more out-of-state students for the sake of the diversity they offer. This attitude, which addresses one of the chief problems of state institutions, is unusual for a state university.

The University of Utah is mainly a commuter campus, with only 15 percent of all students living in dormitories. Approximately 150 honors students live in the UTE wing of one dormitory with regular students who have attained a high GPA. "UTE" stands for "Undergraduate Trend of Excellence," but of course it also suggests the Native-American tribe after which the State of Utah was named. Successful out-of-state applicants are guaranteed housing on campus.

The University of Utah is well endowed with scholarship money. Twenty percent of entering honors freshmen receive an Honors-at-Entrance scholarship, which is a one-year tuition waiver for Utah residents. A smaller number receive Presidential Scholarships, which are free rides for four years. Underscoring its commitment to diversity, the university also offers 22 full four-year scholarships and several partial scholarships to out-of-state students. The Honors Program itself has several scholarships that are given to honors students who have established a good record of achievement.

The University of Utah is a real sleeper. It is a strong secular institution in a deeply religious state, and it offers the best of both worlds: a broad education in a disciplined setting. The Honors Program is structured and strongly front-loaded with western civilization courses, and the emphasis on calculus addresses a significant shortcoming of U.S. higher education. If the program has a weakness, it is tokenism in its foreign language requirement; however, it is one of the few honors programs that even has such a requirement. Overall, the University of Utah offers a very strong honors program. ■

UNIVERSITY OF VIRGINIA

PROGRAM:	Echols Scholars Program
DIRECTOR:	Dean Charles Vandersee
ASSOCIATE DIRECTOR:	Dr. Lynn Davis
ADDRESS:	Echols Scholars Program Garrett Hall University of Virginia Charlottesville, VA 22906
TELEPHONE:	(804) 924-3350
TUITION (FEES):	IN-STATE OUT-OF-STATE $4,330 ($706) $12,254 ($706)
TOWN & CAMPUS:	Excellent
INTELLECTUAL SETTING:	Excellent
ENTRANCE REQUIREMENTS:	Very Competitive
PROGRAM QUALITY:	Good
OVERALL EVALUATION:	★ ★ ★

▶ The University of Virginia (UVA) offers one of the nation's best campus environments. The original campus was designed by Thomas Jefferson to embody his ideals for the university he thought the new nation needed. UVA is a public university that maintains high standards of admission and performance, and it goes virtually without saying that intellectual life at all levels—students, faculty, outside speakers—is excellent.

All of which raises the question whether UVA needs an honors program at all. Like SUNY Binghamton UVA could easily argue that it does not need an honors program because the level of education on campus is already high. And at least in a technical sense, UVA does not have an honors program, but instead has a number of "special programs": The Jefferson Scholars Program is limited to 18 to 20 new students each year and provides a generous stipend, the Rodman Scholars Program serves students majoring in Engineering, and the Echols Scholars

Program, which is the only one covered in this report, supports students in the liberal arts and sciences and is the largest of the three programs.

Entrance to the Echols Scholars Program is based on a set of standards that are unusually flexible. The mean SAT score of students now in the program is 1390, but the program is willing to accept students with substantially lower scores, as much as 150 points lower if such students have demonstrated records of achievement in areas other than test-taking. The Echols Program is, of course, impressed by high school achievement, especially in foreign languages and sciences, but above all the program is looking for the high school student who has shown the self-confidence needed to excel even if it meant risking the GPA.

Also desirable are students who have taken advanced placement courses or done other college-level work; more than 80 percent of the entering fall 1991 class had such credit when they entered UVA. The Echols Program wants responsible students, capable of meaningfully using a good deal of freedom, and advanced placement credit gained while still in high school is one way of demonstrating this.

The Echols Scholars Program is not structured in a technical sense. In fact, it is the absence of conventional undergraduate curriculum structure that distinguishes the program. Students are judged to be sufficiently mature and responsible to be released from conventional undergraduate requirements, including the major, leaving an Echols Scholar free to construct a program suitable to his or her own needs and interests. Unless one believes that responsible and mature undergraduates can be completely self-directed, an excellent advisement system is the order of the day. Entering first-year students create their own programs, and their initial course selections are reviewed by dormitory counselors, faculty advisors, and the dean himself. But in keeping with the philosophy of this program, advising is changed radically after the first year. It moves outside the program into the departments.

Given the absence of curricular structure and the limited nature of the advising program, housing takes on added significance, for it is here that peer relationships can thrive. Thomas Jefferson wanted to create an "academical village," and the Echols Scholars Program is arguably the visible embodiment of this ideal. All Echols freshmen live and work together in two residence halls, Watson House and Maupin House, but only in the first year.

There is no housing shortage on campus, and the only real difficulty is getting a room on "the Lawn," which is the area in front of Jefferson's rotunda. We are told that after the first year, most UVA students have no desire to continue living in campus housing, but those who do find the upperclass dorms relatively quiet. It is the first-year dorms that are noisy.

What are the demographics of Jefferson's academical village? About 800 students are in the Echols Scholars Program, and this is said to amount to about 9 percent of all undergraduates at UVA. Roughly 165 to 175 new freshmen are admitted each year, and although the gender breakdown is normal, there is an unusually large number of out-of-state students, no doubt reflecting UVA's fame. More than 25 percent of students are from out of state, for the most part from east coast and southern states.

Tuition is high at UVA, especially for out-of-state students, and unfortunately UVA has no merit scholarship program. Instead, deserving and qualified students are offered a package of benefits including grants, loans, and work opportunities, a situation that puts UVA at a decided competitive disadvantage.

The Echols Scholars Program at the University of Virginia is a unique opportunity, and we mean this literally. It cannot easily be compared to other honors programs because its philosophy is not replicated elsewhere. Its lack of front-loaded structure is not compensated for by the hidden structure of a strong advisement program. It presupposes a student not only intelligent and assertive but also unusually responsible. It also seems to us to have other flaws, such as the lack of communal housing and an intense honors advisement program after the freshman year, but we could easily be wrong in this perception. Its great strength is the excellence both of UVA and the students themselves, and this may be quite enough. ■

University of Washington

Program:	Honors Program
Director:	Prof. Stevan Harreld
Associate Director:	Dr. Randolph Hennis
Address:	Arts & Sciences Honors Program University of Washington Seattle, WA 98195
Telephone:	(206) 543-7444

Tuition (Fees):	**IN-STATE** $2,532 ($60)	**OUT-OF-STATE** $7,134 ($60)

Town & Campus:	Fair
Intellectual Setting:	Fair
Entrance Requirements:	Competitive
Program Quality:	Good
Overall Evaluation:	★★

▶ The University of Washington (UW) lies just outside Seattle, which determines much that goes on at this school. First, UW is mainly a commuter school, a situation that lends an impersonal feeling to the campus. Secondly, UW is a research-oriented university, and as is often the case in such institutions, undergraduates are treated as second-class citizens and are made to pay the price of their status by attending the huge lecture sections of core courses. In contrast to California and, more recently, Oregon, Washington State has not felt the pinch of the economic recession, so UW has not been forced to downsize. UW is not a great setting for an honors program, but it is a sound one.

Entrance requirements to the honors program are competitive and not very flexible. The stated expectations are a high school GPA of 3.8 and an SAT of 1200. The statistics for this year's incoming freshman class were higher, with an average high school GPA of 3.9 and an SAT of 1300. Furthermore, this was the case even though for many admittees UW was a second choice. Of 275 students admitted to the honors program, only 146 chose to enroll.

UNIVERSITY OF WASHINGTON

The University of Washington operates on a quarter system, with three regular quarters and a summer school as the fourth quarter. A total of 180 credits are needed to graduate, in contrast to the conventional 128-credit total at a normal two-term semester system. This should be kept in mind when looking at the credit requirements of the UW Honors Program.

Honors students are exempt from the regular 60-credit core requirement so that they can take small sections in a demanding honors curriculum. For each of the first three years, honors students take three five-credit, year-long honors courses in Western Civilization, World Civilization, and Natural Science, for a total of 45 credits (15 credits yearly) that make up the heart of the Honors Program. In conjunction with these, students take a five-credit writing lab designed to develop their analytical writing skills. Finally, students take at least five credits selected from among several advanced seminars. The basic honors requirement is thus 55 credits, or nearly one-third of the academic experience at UW.

In addition, students are expected to complete departmental honors programs in their majors, and as standards vary from major to major, no specific requirements are stated. Normally, students earn from 12 to 15 honors credits in their majors, which usually involves doing a senior thesis as well. Students who complete both the General Studies Curriculum and departmental honors receive a degree "With College Honors." Those who do only departmental honors graduate "With Distinction." No transcript notation made for students who do basic but not departmental honors. Incoming freshmen should therefore be aware that nearly 40 percent of their undergraduate careers will be spent in honors programs. It is expected that students will maintain an overall 3.3 GPA to graduate with honors and never drop below 3.0 in any academic quarter.

Out-of-state tuition at UW is $7,134 annually, and in-state tuition is $2,532. A small number of full-tuition scholarships are available to honors students, as are a large number of smaller scholarships. Program authorities say that honors students are likely to do well in the general scholarship competition as well, and UW offers a large number of scholarships.

There is no special housing reserved for honors students at UW, and program authorities say there is no demand for such housing. Some honors students live in regular dormitories with about 7,000 other resident students; others live in fraternities or sororities, in rented apartments, or at home. They are said to be happy with that arrangement. It should also be noted that there are no extracurricular activities specifically for honors students, and this too is said to be to the satisfaction of the honors students.

The University of Washington Honors Program enrolls between 120 and 150 students per year, with a total enrollment of nearly 900. Of this number, 50 percent are women and 10 percent are minorities, including about 10 African-Americans, 10 Native Americans and Hispanics, and 80 Asian-Americans. The number of out-of-state students is low—only about 15 percent—most of whom come from the other two west coast states. This makes sense in light of California's size and budget constraints, and it reflects one of the more significant trends in west coast demographics, the northward migration of the professional class. Interestingly, Washington is also getting students from Oregon in increasing numbers, a phenomenon that can be explained by the weaker Oregon economy.

The University of Washington Honors Program is very good. Its only significant disadvantage is the large impersonal university that houses it. The program itself is excellent because it is strongly front-loaded, and not at the expense of the upperclass years. Also to be considered is Seattle, boating on Puget Sound, and hiking or mountain climbing in Olympic National Park. ∎

WEST VIRGINIA UNIVERSITY

PROGRAM:	The Honors Program
DIRECTOR:	Dr. William E. Collins
STAFF ASSOCIATE:	Mrs. JoAnn Evans
ADDRESS:	The WVU Honors Program West Virginia University PO Box 6635 Morgantown, WV 26506-6635
TELEPHONE:	(304) 293-2100
TUITION (FEES):	**IN-STATE** $1,470 ($280) **OUT-OF-STATE** $5,314 ($410)
TOWN & CAMPUS:	Fair
INTELLECTUAL SETTING:	Fair
ENTRANCE REQUIREMENTS:	Competitive
PROGRAM QUALITY:	Good
OVERALL EVALUATION:	★

▶ West Virginia University (WVU) is mainly a residential school, and it services a socially mixed student body in a heavily working-class state. It is a solid but not inspiring place. The university attracts a large number of students from neighboring states because of its low tuition. Morgantown is not an intellectual and cultural mecca, and if anything there rules supreme, it is Big East football. However, the surrounding countryside is beautiful.

Entrance requirements to the WVU Honors Program are competitive. An applicant must have one of three combinations of test score and high school GPA: The first is an SAT score of at least 1160 (or an ACT score of 28) combined with a GPA of 3.8, the second is an SAT score of at least 1290 (or an ACT score of 31) combined with a GPA of 3.5, and the third is National Merit Semifinalist status combined with a 3.5 GPA. In short, one may compensate for a lower high school GPA with a higher test score, or vice versa. The average SAT for entering honors freshmen is 1230.

In addition, applicants are required to submit two essays of 250 words each on topics specified by the program. The purpose of these essays is to assess motivation for honors study and to help the staff become acquainted with the applicants. Students must first apply for admission to the university, and although there is no deadline for this, honors housing is in short supply and applicants are encouraged to apply early.

The requirements for the WVU Honors Program are relatively simple. To graduate as a University Honors Scholar, students must have completed a minimum of 24 hours of designated honors courses. Within this general framework, there are specific requirements: at least three and no more than six credits must be earned through an independent study project carried out during a summer, and three credits must be earned in a senior seminar. No more than nine of the minimum 24 credits may be earned from the same academic department.

Six honors credits (three per semester) may be earned by participation in an approved study-abroad program. The favored program is at the University of Leeds in England, although WVU is able to make arrangements with other British universities. Five percent of WVU honors students participate in these programs.

To remain in the program, students must maintain a cumulative GPA of 3.2 over the first 28 earned credits, 3.3 for 29 to 88 earned credits, and 3.4 for 89 or more earned credits. In other words, the standard is ratcheted upwards over the undergraduate career. Students must also take at least 12 hours per semester. Those who do not meet these criteria are put on probation for one semester and then dismissed if they do not come up to standard.

There are some specific extracurricular honors activities at WVU. Entering freshmen attend a retreat on the Saturday before classes begin, where they meet upperclassmen and faculty who will be teaching that year. During the first semester, there are additional orientation classes for freshmen. For all honors students there are occasional out-of-town trips to concerts and museums. Annual weekend trips to New York City or Washington or another large city are offered. There are also trips to nearby Pittsburgh for cultural events. Occasional dinners and small group meetings are held in Stalnaker Hall and in the Martha C. Howard Honors Lounge.

WVU is mainly a residential school, and housing is provided for honors students. All freshmen are assigned to suites on the honors floor of Stalnaker Hall. Most upperclass honors students find their own accommodations after the first year, although some remain in Stalnaker Hall.

Financial aid is available on the basis of need, and honors students should be in an especially competitive position. Honors students receiving no other financial aid qualify for a $250 annual scholarship, renewable for four years if the student remains in good standing in the honors program.

There are 700 students in the WVU Honors Program, with approximately 130 freshmen entering the program each year. Of the total enrollment, 55 percent are women, about 2 percent are minorities, and of the latter category, fewer than five are African-Americans. About 18 percent of the honors students are from out of state, mainly from nearby Pennsylvania, New Jersey, and Maryland.

The WVU Honors Program is not front-loaded, and so there is no outstanding advantage to being in the program for freshmen. The university is in a beautiful location, but it is most certainly not one of America's intellectual centers. The Honors Program is well managed and has no weak spots, and the university is a tuition bargain by any standards. ■

COLLEGE OF WILLIAM & MARY

PROGRAM:	James Monroe Scholar Program
DIRECTOR:	Prof. Joel D. Schwartz
ASSISTANT DIRECTOR:	Ms. Lisa Grimes
ADDRESS:	Prof. Joel D. Schwartz Director, Roy R. Charles Center Williamsburg, VA 23187-8795
TELEPHONE:	(804) 221-2460
TUITION (FEES):	**IN-STATE** $4,414 (incl.) **OUT-OF-STATE** $12,604 (incl.)
TOWN & CAMPUS:	Good
INTELLECTUAL SETTING:	Good
ENTRANCE REQUIREMENTS:	Very Competitive
PROGRAM QUALITY:	Fair
OVERALL EVALUATION:	★ ★

▶ With 5,000 students, the College of William & Mary is not only one of the nation's oldest colleges, it is also a state university, even though it does not look like one. It gets roughly 45 percent of its funding from the state of Virginia. The campus is set next to Colonial Williamsburg, which was renovated in the 1920s with money from the Ford Motor Company. It has similar architecture and was already more than 50 years old when Thomas Jefferson attended as a student, years before the American Revolution. Such a setting is not to everyone's taste, and it is very definitely not the usual setting for a state university.

William & Mary is a fine school, attracting some of the best qualified high school graduates from Virginia and the South. The surrounding countryside is a treasure trove of American history, especially from the colonial period and the time of the Civil War. The faculty is very good, and outside speakers and good extracurricular activities are common. The intellectual setting is traditional and of high quality.

Entrance requirements to the James Monroe Scholar Program are very competitive. Prospective honors students first apply to the

College of William & Mary and then are selected from the general pool of successful applicants. The program wants "exceptional" high school records, which translates into a minimum class standing in the top 5 percent and SAT or ACT scores in at least the 95th percentile, which is said to mean 1400 on the SAT. The average SAT score of this year's entering class is 1410.

The program is rather minimal. First-year students take conventional core requirements and in addition are urged to take at least one honors course. These courses, which are never required, have from 10 to 15 students and are writing, reading, and discussion intensive. In the 1993 fall semester several sections of a course on middle eastern culture were given, and the offering for the spring 1994 semester was a course (in several sections) on community and authority in western traditions.

One of the benefits of the James Monroe Scholar Program is a guaranteed summer scholarship of $2,000 to enable the student to conduct independent research that is "intellectually broadening." The money is to be used between the junior and senior years and may but need not be used to support a project in the student's major. Most students receiving these awards incorporate international travel into their plans and most do creative work.

A major feature of the program is a strong selection of extracurricular activities. Discounted tickets are provided for the Williamsburg theater, and special talks and lunches are organized for James Monroe Scholars. Many guest speakers to the campus are corralled into doing an extra, more intimate performance with the James Monroe Scholars.

First-year students may elect to live in one of two honors residences, Hunt Hall or Taliaferro Hall. These halls are centrally located next to the Campus Center, and are equipped with microcomputer labs. Most important, first-year students are initiated into academic life in an intimate and enriched living context.

There are 300 James Monroe Scholars at the College of William & Mary, and each year 65 to 105 new freshmen are accepted. Women make up 50 percent of the total, and 10 percent are minorities. Among the minority students are approximately 20 African-Americans and 10 Hispanics. About 50 percent of the students are from out of state, and they come from a variety of distant states, not just neighboring North Carolina, Maryland, Tennessee, and West Virginia.

IVY LEAGUE PROGRAMS AT STATE SCHOOL PRICES

William & Mary is expensive for a state university, so the question of financial aid for James Monroe Scholars is significant. There are no specific merit scholarships, and not all need-based claims for aid can be met. The applicant is therefore forewarned that he or she may have to pay full tuition at William & Mary.

The James Monroe Scholar Program at the College of William & Mary is a singular opportunity that is not easy to compare with conventional state university programs. The program is somewhat thin, but there are compensating factors, not the least of which is the all-around quality of the institution.

Prospective applicants should ask themselves whether they want the conservative surroundings offered by William & Mary. If the answer is yes, then such students should also look at Miami University of Ohio, the University of New Hampshire, and perhaps New College in Florida, which offer comparable settings. In any case, for the student who wants this type of setting, William & Mary is an exquisite choice. ■

UNIVERSITY OF WISCONSIN—MADISON

PROGRAM:	The Honors Program
FACULTY HONORS DIRECTOR:	Dean A. Margaret Elowson
ASSISTANT DIRECTOR:	Dean Patricia K. Fessendon
ADDRESS:	The Honors Program 409 South Hall 1055 Bascom Mall University of Wisconsin Madison, WI 53706
TELEPHONE:	(608) 262-2984
TUITION (FEES):	**IN-STATE** $2,344 (incl.) **OUT-OF-STATE** $7,840 (incl.)
TOWN & CAMPUS:	Excellent
INTELLECTUAL SETTING:	Excellent
ENTRANCE REQUIREMENTS:	Competitive
PROGRAM QUALITY:	Fair
OVERALL EVALUATION:	★

▶ The University of Wisconsin—Madison is large, with 40,000 students, but it has the reputation of being one of the best state universities in the United States. Continuing a one-hundred-year tradition, it is liberal and progressive in spirit, although it is a much different place from the radical center it was during the Vietnam War era. The campus is hilly at the center, alongside Lake Mendota, and fiercely cold in winter. Party life is good, as is intellectual life, and the city of Madison ranks with Berkeley, Ann Arbor, and Cambridge as a quality setting. It is also the state capital.

We are discussing the Honors Program of the College of Letters and Science (L&S), the main program for students interested in liberal arts degrees. There are also honors programs in the School of Nursing, the School of Business, and the College of Agriculture and Life Sciences.

Entrance requirements are competitive but flexible. The brochure states that students should be in the top 10 percent of their high school classes. A minimum score of 1200 on the SAT or 28 on the ACT is expected. One brief essay is required as well. It should be noted that the applicant must meet all of the above requirements. Students with appropriate test scores but from high schools that do not rank their students should apply with a cover letter of explanation and attach a copy of their high school transcript. Students with at least a 3.5 high school GPA and an ACT of greater than 31 or an SAT of greater than 1300 are nominated to join without an essay.

The Honors Program itself is loosely organized and is best looked at from its end point. To graduate with the Honors Degree, a student must have completed at least 40 credits in honors courses and the junior-senior honors curriculum in one major, including a senior thesis, and must have maintained a 3.3 GPA. Regular students may enter the Honors Program laterally as late as their junior year but must complete all honors requirements. Each semester the Honors Program compiles a lengthy list of courses which are either exclusively Honors, open to all students but recommended for Honors, or convertible to Honors with the consent of the instructor.

There are no course distribution requirements for the Honors Degree, but students who opt to do Sophomore Honors must take 20 honors credits in the first two years, nine of which are in humanities, the social sciences, and the natural sciences. This option is entirely voluntary and was instituted to serve students who transfer to professional programs after two years of liberal arts curricula.

The L&S Honors Program is currently in a period of transition. Traditionally, Wisconsin's College of Letters & Science has wanted to have an open, inclusive, and loosely defined honors program. This rationale fits well with the liberal, democratic ideology of the university, but it can also serve to camouflage cost-saving measures on the part of the university or state legislature. Recently, the Letters & Science College has begun moving toward a more tightly organized honors program. They have raised admission standards to attain a better honors student body, and ironically this has resulted in an expanding honors program at the same time that the university is reducing the size of the freshman class. The state legislature has also begun putting more money into the program, so now Wisconsin can offer enough honors courses to begin thinking in terms of requiring them. All in all, the program seems well on the way to improvement.

But it is not there yet. Underclass lecture sections at large state universities are themselves usually large and anonymous, and Wisconsin's are no exception. By not having a front-loaded set of requirements, Wisconsin allows its underclassmen to float, and they are likely to do just that. However, a vigorous program of academic advising is beginning to correct this problem.

The L&S Honors Program has a total of 1,200 students, slightly more women than men, far more in-state (75 percent) than out-of-state (25 percent) students, and a minority representation of less than 5 percent. Dormitory housing, generally lacking in Madison, is no longer a problem because of the recent downsizing of the entering classes. Yet there is still only one reserved honors floor in a dormitory, and with 63 available places, it can hardly accommodate more than a handful of students.

Tuition at the University of Wisconsin is not expensive. For 1993–94, it is $2,344 per year (two semesters) for in-state students and $7,840 per year for out-of-state students. The state legislature has recently added a number of incentive scholarships for in-state students qualified for the Honors Program.

The Wisconsin L&S Honors Program is not excellent, but it is on its way to becoming good. At the moment, it seems to be a good option for a highly motivated, well advised student, but is questionable for a student who needs structure. The strength of doing honors at the College of Letters and Science at the University of Wisconsin is not the program but rather the town, campus, and intellectual setting. They are among the best in America, so whatever the shortcomings of the L&S Honors Program, the experience will still most likely be a good one. ■

UNIVERSITY OF WYOMING

PROGRAM:	Honors Program
DIRECTOR:	Dr. Duncan Harris
ASSOCIATE DIRECTOR:	Ms. Linda White
ADDRESS:	Honors Program Honors Center, Merica Hall University of Wyoming Laramie, WY 82071
TELEPHONE:	(307) 766-4110
TUITION (FEES):	**IN-STATE** $690 ($134) **OUT-OF-STATE** $2,457 ($134)
TOWN & CAMPUS:	Fair
INTELLECTUAL SETTING:	Fair
ENTRANCE REQUIREMENTS:	Easy
PROGRAM QUALITY:	Good
OVERALL EVALUATION:	★

▶ The campus is all right, the town is indifferent, but the surrounding countryside and skyscape are incomparable. The University of Wyoming (UW) is a small (12,000 students) and inexpensive state university that excels in engineering and generally offers a good education. Denver, two hours away, is the closest big city, and the next best thing is Fort Collins, 45 minutes away. Intellectual life is nothing to write home about.

Entrance requirements to the Honors Program are both competitive and not especially demanding: UW looks for a minimum high school GPA of 3.7, which is the equivalent of a solid A−, *or* at least a 28 on the ACT, which according to Wyoming authorities is about an 1190 on the SAT. The average ACT score of current students is 29. The point is that one need meet only one of these requirements. Once again, it is helpful to remember the essentials of the politics of college admissions. Rural kids do well on grades but less well on tests, and the opposite is the case with big-city kids. Girls do better on grades than on tests. Wyoming has found the way to keep everybody happy: require one or the other.

The Honors Program itself is structured throughout the four undergraduate years. In the freshman year, everyone takes a six-credit *Freshman Colloquium*, a one-year western civilization course that emphasizes analytical reading, writing, and discussion. The second year involves a three-credit *Non-Western Perspectives* course, emphasizing the experience of African, Asian, or American-Indian peoples. The third year involves another three-credit course, called *Modes of Understanding*, which focuses on knowledge in a selected area of academic thought. Finally, the senior year experience is organized around a three-credit *Senior Honors Seminar*, which focuses on a complex social issue and attempts to analyze it from different perspectives.

All of these courses are given in multiple sections. Ten freshman sections were given in 1993–94, as well as several sections of sophomore, junior, and senior courses. These are small, with no more than 20 students in freshman sections and even fewer in the subsequent sections. All are taught by full-time, competitively selected faculty.

In addition to the five courses (most of which, by the way, also fulfill university or college requirements), honors students write a senior honors paper based on independent research. Most often the research is done in the area of a student's major and supervised by a faculty member in that discipline, but occasionally a biochemistry student puts together a book of poems or a geologist investigates early exploration in Wyoming. Some funding is available to support this research.

There are 350 honors students at the University of Wyoming, and each year's freshman class has roughly 90 students. Most of these (75 percent) come from Wyoming, and are primarily from middle-class backgrounds. Out-of-state students mainly come from neighboring Colorado, Montana, and Nebraska. Women make up roughly 50 percent of the honors student body, and minorities (all Hispanics) comprise only 1 percent. There are four foreign students currently in the program.

Reserved for students in the Honors Program are 72 merit-based honors stipends that cover in-state tuition. Many other departmental and university scholarships are held by students in the program.

Housing at the University of Wyoming is adequate, and there is an honors floor in White Hall, where approximately 75 honors students live. Other honors students live in one of the four other undergraduate dormitories or in Laramie.

IVY LEAGUE PROGRAMS AT STATE SCHOOL PRICES

The Honors Program at the University of Wyoming is not exciting, but it is sound. It provides a core of small courses for four years and enables students to avoid some of the large lecture sections. The student body is fairly homogeneous, however, and intellectual life is not as dynamic as one might hope. ■

ARCO

"HOW TO" GUIDES

How to Develop and Write a Research Paper
How to Read and Write About Drama
How to Read and Write About Fiction
How to Read and Interpret Poetry
How to Write Book Reports
How to Write Poetry
How To Write Short Stories
How to Write Themes and Essays
How to Write a Thesis

AVAILABLE AT BOOKSTORES EVERYWHERE

ARCO
BOOKS FOR GRADUATE SCHOOL AND BEYOND

ARCO'S SUPERCOURSES

GMAT SuperCourse
GRE SuperCourse
LSAT SuperCourse
MCAT SuperCourse
TOEFL SuperCourse

TOEFL

TOEFL: Test of English as a Foreign Language
TOEFL Grammar Workbook
TOEFL Reading and Vocabulary Workbook
TOEFL Skills for Top Scores

ARCO'S CRAM COURSES

GMAT Cram Course
GRE Cram Course
LSAT Cram Course

TEACHER CERTIFICATION

CBEST: California Educational Basic Skills Test
NTE: National Teacher Examinations
PPST: Pre-Professional Skills Tests
Teacher Certification Tests

HEALTH PROFESSIONS

Allied Health Professions
Nursing School Entrance Examinations
PCAT: Pharmacy College Admission Test

GRADUATE SCHOOL GUIDES

The Best Law Schools
Getting into Law School: Strategies for the 90's
Getting into Medical School: Strategies for the 90's
The Grad Student's Guide to Getting Published

GRADUATE & PROFESSIONAL SCHOOL ENTRANCE

GMAT: Graduate Management Admission Test
GRE: Graduate Record Examination
GRE • GMAT Math Review
Graduate Record Examination in Computer Science
Graduate Record Examination in Engineering
Graduate Record Examination in Psychology
GRE • LSAT Logic Workbook
LSAT: Law School Admission Test
MAT: Miller Analogies Test
MCAT Sample Exams

AVAILABLE AT BOOKSTORES EVERYWHERE